this book was given to:

_____

from:

_____

date:

_____

slow growth

equals

strong roots

*finding grace, freedom, and purpose
in an overachieving world*

MARY MARANTZ

Revell

a division of *Baker Publishing* Group
Grand Rapids, Michigan

© 2022 by Mary Marantz

Published by Revell
a division of Baker Publishing Group
PO Box 6287, Grand Rapids, MI 49516-6287
www.revellbooks.com

Printed in the United States of America

Library of Congress Cataloging-in-Publication Data
Names: Marantz, Mary, author.
Title: Slow growth equals strong roots : finding grace, freedom, and purpose in an overachieving world / Mary Marantz.
Description: Grand Rapids, MI : Revell, a division of Baker Publishing Group, [2022]
Identifiers: LCCN 2021023643 | ISBN 9780800738464 (cloth) | ISBN 9781493434329 (ebook)
Subjects: LCSH: Christian life. | Simplicity—Religious aspects—Christianity. | LCGFT: Essays.
Classification: LCC BV4510.3 .M335 2022 | DDC 248.4—dc23
LC record available at https://lccn.loc.gov/2021023643

Some material has been excerpted from Mary Marantz, *Dirt: Growing Strong Roots in What Makes the Broken Beautiful* (Revell, 2020).

Published in association with Illuminate Literary Agency, www.illuminateliterary.com

Principal photography by Justin Marantz and Mary Marantz.

Additional photography on pages 28–29, 36–37, 49, 57, 60–61, 68–69, 84–85, 129, 143, 189, 211, 231, 244, 262, 265, 294, 296–97 by Abby Grace Photography.

Additional photography on pages 96, 277 by Daphne & Dean Photography.

Interior design by William Overbeeke.

22 23 24 25 26 27 28   7 6 5 4 3 2 1

TO JUSTIN,
*who was the first one
to ever tell me
slow growth equals strong roots.*

And TO KIM,
*who made me believe in the power
of standing firm
in our place on the shore.*

THANK YOU BOTH
*for being the anchors
in my high-wire act
of a life.*

contents

Slow growth equals strong roots.

THE AUTHOR

THIS IS ULTIMATELY a book about breaking free from achieving for your worth.

But what I want you to know right off the bat, is that these words are not being handed down to you from some mountaintop moment bathed in golden light. One where I have all the answers and pretend to have never again struggled with comparison or feeling like not enough of something to be invited into most rooms.

This book was written from the trenches.

It was birthed from a place of deep exhaustion and daily desperation. A feeling that a life spent chasing the next dopamine hit of a gold-star high, only to feel more empty with every checkmark that seemed to numb but never satisfy . . . was, in fact, no kind of life at all. These words are an

NOTE

*read this
before you turn
the next page . . .*

anthology and a twisting road map. A collective
charted course of a grown woman just trying to
find her way to freedom.

When I wrote my first book, *Dirt*, I called it a
love letter to The Girl in the Trailer. In so many
ways, this book is a love letter to The Girl After
the Trailer, the woman I affectionately call "The
Most Put-Together Woman in the Room." She
has run so hard for so long trying to get that lit-
tlest version of herself to safety, that she doesn't
know how to stop. And in all this trying to outrun failure she has now built a life so beautiful
on the outside, you would never guess the hard
things she has had to overcome.

I want you to know that I get the irony of
making a book like this so . . . well . . . *pretty* on

the outside. Between the pink and gold, the typography and beautiful pictures, in so many ways this book is the most put-together version of itself.

That was on purpose.

This is the book I would have picked up five years ago when I was at the height of achieving for my worth. I would have been drawn to it for how it looked, how it fit into the beautiful life I was trying so hard to build. But my hope is that once I got home and opened it up, I would have been changed by the message inside. That is my hope for you too. That however this book found its way to you, all the pretty of these pages you now hold will pale in comparison to the beauty of what God does with these words in your heart.

As you go through, you will be introduced to different (yet somehow all the same) versions of The Most Put-Together Woman in the Room. These characters are the people we think we have to become in order to belong. You'll meet The Woman Who Is Always Performing, The High-Wire Tightrope Walker, The Contortionist, The Masquerader, and The Illusionist in the Distance.

What's interesting for you to know, though, is that the editorial images of these characters you now find in these pages are all photos that my husband Justin and I took over five years ago. We were starting to find ourselves in a place of burnout with our photography business, and we wanted to create something just for us. So we set up the ballerina shoot and a styled shoot in Venice with a few different looks that was a total dream come true. But then we came home from that trip and only edited up a few favorites and quickly posted them to Instagram. The ultimate in highlight reels. And that was it. Nothing else was ever done with those photos. They remained unpublished for years, just sitting and waiting for the decisive moment.

And then this book happened. And it suddenly felt like maybe God had a plan for these images all along, as all the different puzzle pieces snapped into place for the story we were telling. Which brings me to the other interesting thing for you to know about these editorial images: every single one of them is of the same model—our friend Kathryn, who was kind enough to help us out. So when I say these characters you'll meet are different yet somehow all the same versions of The Most Put-Together Woman in the Room... I mean it, *literally*.

When I was talking to my friend and coach, Kim, about whether we were crazy to use such high-fashion, editorial images in a book about letting go of being perfect, she said something that stopped me in my tracks:

> The very fact that you created these images five years ago when you were at the height of your achieving, is exactly why they are such a necessary photo narrative for this book. See, you just thought you were creating something pretty. At that time in your life, you thought *this*— being masked, always performing, staying on your toes, wearing all the pretty clothes— was how to be beautiful to the world. So you put together styled shoots of what you thought the world wanted to see. But at the very same time, you were reaching that breaking point of burnout, that pain of being masked and always trying so hard to be perfect. And you see that in those photos—you *feel* it— that tension there of the woman who is always performing now trying to break free. That's what makes them so powerful. It's the fact that you didn't even know at the time just how much the woman in those photos was you.

What follows in these pages is a journey of unraveling, this coming undone to striving, achieving, and perfection in pursuit of grace, freedom, and purpose.

And it's for every woman who has grown weary of the performance. ▦

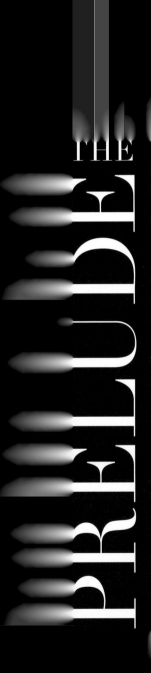

THE PRELUDE

AT A CERTAIN POINT, *you stop running.*

Breathless and at last exhausted, you double over at the pain of a lifetime spent proving. You've run so hard for so long, you've gone so far out into the world, only to keep finding yourself back at the beginning. You have spent a lifetime starting over, breaking loose to run free only to be taken captive again and again. This one truth always dragging, always clawing at your heels like the heavy chains you never asked to bear: no matter how hard you run, you can't outrun you.

So you crawl there for a while, panting through the pain, and then you curl up in surrender and rest your face on the cool, hard ground. Death to this old life you once knew. A mourning of what was lost before the thrill of hope takes flight. A dying of self to become a new thing—this time one with both roots and wings.

"God set me free, of me."

—THE BOOK *Dirt*

THE INCITING

OUR STORY BEGINS, as all great stories do, with our inciting incident.

The *inciting incident* is a darling in the literary tool belt amongst most writers both for setting in motion the telling of a powerful story . . . and also for occasionally sounding smart at cocktail parties. Trust me on this. If someone asks what you do for a living over passed champagne and miniature pigs in a blanket in the middle of some stranger-once-removed's living room, you could fumble out something like, "Words. I write words. Words are my friends. Occasionally people read them." But I assure you it sounds much more impressive if you can instead wax poetic about the moment something happens that divides our beloved protagonist's life into *Before*

INCIDENT

and *After*. My friend Hannah Brencher calls that moment a Sharpie mark slashing through the calendar.

We are all just one Sharpie mark away from having our lives forever divided in two.

But if you're looking for an official definition, which you probably are, it would go something like this: "The inciting incident is an episode, plot point or event that hooks the reader into the story. This particular moment is when an event thrusts the protagonist into the main action" of the narrative arc,* one which hopefully will leave her utterly and forever changed by the end.

We are standing on the precipice of our *After*.

*"Inciting Incident: Definition, Tips, and Examples," Now Novel, https://www.nownovel.com/blog/inciting-incident/.

It is this moment when we decide we have reached the end of something. We have reached the end of all this striving. All this hustling. All this achieving for our worth. We keep hoping against hope that the next gold star will finally be the one to fill this giant hole we've had in our hearts for as long as we can remember. Except if third grade taught us anything, it's that even a whole sheet full of gold stars is still razor thin when you turn it to the side. Trying to fill that hole in your heart would take nothing short of a *blizzard* of gilded five-prong snowflakes. And you are a person who has grown weary of living in the storm.

You are dust. You are embers. You are walking around so bone-tired and world-wearied, it's like one big raw nerve ending screaming out every time someone carelessly bumps into you. You are burned-out, there is no question. But what you've realized more than anything is that the burn didn't make you any harder on the outside like you thought it would, this charred, petrified block of wood made impenetrable by walking through the fire.

Instead you have been reduced to this brittle, fragile, ashes-to-ashes version of yourself. You have run so far for so long, trying to achieve your way into worth, that you are completely spent. Consumed. Exhausted. Finished. You're doing everything you can to hold it all together, but every day you're out there these little pieces of you keep flying away. Pieces you know you can never get back. They float away, never once turning around to give any indication that they are going

OUR INCITING INCIDENT IS THIS:
"BREATHLESS AND AT LAST
EXHAUSTED."

to miss you half as much as you already miss them. It's gotten to where you feel like at the slightest push, the slightest gentle breeze, you might just disappear altogether.

Dust on the wind.

Our inciting incident is this: "Breathless and *at last exhausted*."

We don't get to our Sharpie-mark moment unless you are starting to hit that point where you have finally had enough. Until you are ready to trade all this striving, achieving, and performing, caught in an endless pursuit of gold stars and outward success. Until you are finally starting to realize that maybe there is no amount of more that will ever keep you from feeling less-than.

Are you right in the middle of your own doubled-over-at-the-pain-of-a-lifetime-spent-proving moment? Do you wish for nothing more than to curl up in surrender and rest your face on the cool, hard ground? Have you tired yourself out yet only to end up back where you started? Have you gone hard enough and long enough that you are *at last* exhausted?

Are you ready to stop all this running from your own story yet?

Good. Now the real work can begin. ▨

breaking
GRO

PART I

UND

this time we have is fleeting

№ 1

WALK AMONG
THE FIREFLIES

the antidote to more is noticing all we already have

And amazement
seized them all,
and they glorified God
and were filled with awe,
saying, "We have seen
extraordinary things today."

LUKE 5:26

I'M NOT SURE WHERE all the fireflies have gone.

When I was little—a gap-toothed, skinned-knees
mess of curly brown hair—growing up this wild thing,
untamed, on the top of Fenwick Mountain, there was
no shortage of fireflies. *Lightning bugs*, as we used to
call them. On those hottest July nights when the tall
pines on the edge of our neighbor's yard blurred and
bled into one another—this twisted tangle of stark,
bare arms, these puppet masters pulling all the strings
and casting shadows of our most-feared demons
against the deep blue fade of twilight giving way to
the darkness—our whole world could be seen by the
light of a million fireflies. Like a fluorescent night-light
protecting us from all the monsters hiding in the shadows. An Appalachian allegory of the cave, lighting up

23

these mere reflections of the versions of ourselves we might one day become.

We would sit like that for hours—leaning back and propped up on the palms of our as-yet unscarred hands, the blades of thick, freshly cut crabgrass stabbing at the backs of our knees—telling ghost stories against the silhouette of imagined apparitions that were never really there. A million points of light blinking in and out of our existence. As if one day we might just disappear right alongside them.

I'm forty as I write this. And for years I've watched the summers pass without the slightest glimpse of that electric neon yellow burning up the night sky. Where there used to be a million miracles, now it can be hard to see even one.

Growing up tends to do that to us.

Somewhere among the mortgage payments and stainless-steel appliances, the retirement funds and the endless piles of laundry, we lose that wonder for a life we have spent a lifetime dreaming of. I used to sit with a blue spiral-bound notebook outside the trailer where I grew up in West Virginia, drawing sketches and dreaming of the *real* house I would one day have. Now all I'm tempted to see is a kitchen that needs updating, perpetually dirty dishes, and a boiler in the basement

> *BECOMING AN ADULT TENDS TO PUT BLINDERS ON US. IT MAKES US FORGET TO SEE THE THINGS RIGHT IN FRONT OF US THAT USED TO GIVE US WONDER.*

that—if all its coughs and sputterings are any indication—we're going to need to replace pretty soon.

We lose ourselves in our obligations and color-coded to-do lists. We feel tired all the time. We drink more wine than maybe we should. Food has started to lose all its flavor. And we just let the episodes run on the latest binge-worthy television show, one after another after another, until all the plotlines blur. We're numb. We're checked out of our own lives.

And we're not even sure we would recognize that wild-thing, un-tamed version of ourselves if she came and sat down on the couch beside us with her skinned knees and tangled hair, looked us right in our exhausted eyes that are mirror reflections of her own, and asked the question we've been asking ourselves for far too long now:

"What happened to you?"

I once heard a photographer named Will Jacks say, "Be willing to walk among the fireflies." When he said that, I took it to mean be willing to slow down, be willing to walk in wonder, be willing to see the smallest things right in front of you as the miracles they really are.

Becoming an adult tends to put blinders on us. It makes us forget to see the things right in front of us that used to give us wonder. The things that used to give us pause.

And it got me thinking: what if fireflies cease to exist in equal and opposite proportion to the amount of time you spend noticing them? It reminds me of Julia Roberts with her pixie cut and fairy wings in *Hook*, telling all the children to clap if they believe. But never once letting on just how much other people's clapping was a lifeline for her.

Without it, she didn't know how to breathe.

For years I wasn't sure where all the fireflies in my life had gone.

But then two summers ago, in the year of our Lord 2020, when the world was burning down all around us, for the first time in a long time . . . the fireflies returned. The first time it happened we were sitting a

It takes a radical act of

COURAGE

to see the miracle in the mundane.

socially distant six feet apart on our front porch with our friends Erin and Peter. And we all had to blink our eyes against the night sky to believe what we were seeing.

Just like that, in the height of darkness . . . the light returned.

I don't know why the fireflies chose to come back in a year that was so hard. If I were them, I think I would have just stayed floating safely on warm currents of air to far-off places like Neverland or maybe Bora Bora, sailing off in a deep blue sea of dreams. Maybe they returned because the world got quiet enough that it finally felt safe for wonder to re-emerge. Maybe they were like the dolphins that supposedly were swimming in the Venice canals because the dust had settled and the water had become clear again. Or maybe, just maybe, it's because we were all slowed down enough to begin this act of *noticing* again.

Noticing the smallest things right in front of us for the wonder and the miracle that they really are.

It takes a radical act of courage to see beauty among the broken. But it is no less radical or courageous to witness the miracle among the mundane.

Perhaps this is the antidote to the problem of more: it's noticing the magic and enough-ness of all that we already have.

So we begin this good work right here.

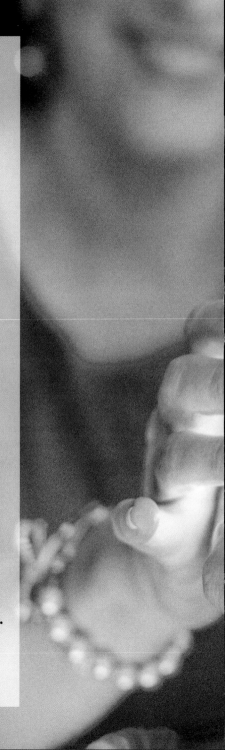

SLOW GROWTH PRAYER

GOD,

I don't want to wake up one day and realize I've sleepwalked through my entire life.

I don't want to spend another day pretending like every little piece of this life in front of me is anything less than extraordinary.

This blue planet floating through space, spinning wildly on its axis.

7.8 billion humans.

And somehow you still see fit to bring me my people.

You care enough to give me a house and sunsets, the smell of salt air, a song that can bring me right back to my childhood, fluffy dogs and cold tangerines.

I want to see every good gift from above for the miracle it really is.

Wake me up, God.

Help me to not miss it.

Oh, how I am so afraid I'm missing it.

AMEN.

№ 2

A TOSSED AND
TURBULENT SEA

let the wind howl and the storms rage—
God is the rock that won't be moved

But let him ask in faith without doubting. For the doubter is like the surging sea, driven and tossed by the wind. That person should not expect to receive anything from the Lord, being double-minded and unstable in all his ways.

JAMES 1:6–8 CSB

I'VE ALWAYS WANTED to be one of those people who are *unshakable*. Unflappable. The Unsinkable Molly Brown. The kind of person who seems to have built their life upon an unwavering, rock-solid stance, their feet always planted shoulder-width apart, heels rooted firmly in the cold, hard ground beneath them. Their heads held high, spiraling ever upward toward the heavens. Their eyes fixed on something even higher that no one else around them can ever seem to see.

They don't care when the storms rage, when the winds howl, when the wolves are scratching at the door. They pay no mind to the disappointing setbacks, the down-to-the-buzzer losses, the times when they find themselves in the unenviable position of being forced *yet again* to start over from the beginning. They do not grow weary of doing good when they lose their grip or lose their way and the boulder rolls all the way back down the mountain. They simply straighten their back, set their jaw, and begin the long, slow climb once again.

Equally, they remain unchanged when things *do* go their way. When the ship comes in, when the wind falls, when good fortune comes knocking at the door dressed in a cloak and wrapped in an enigma—the only mystery being how long she intends to stay this time. She can come or she can go. She can smile her lucky smile or turn a cold, indifferent shoulder.

Whatever happens, such people simply remain. Steadfast. And *solid*.

Let me be clear. I have *never* been that person.

I have always been more like a high-wire tightrope walker, her confidence built upon the thin, fleeting air buoying up beneath her. These billowing currents of hot air and highlight reels turned icy chill in the fickle fog of their absence, leaving tiny thunderstorms of destruction in their wake. She's up and she's down and she's everywhere in between. She could be *falling* or she could be *flying*—the thrill of both those words ever-present on her lips and never really knowing which one. That is the rip cord that somehow keeps her tethered. Leaping, always leaping, never really knowing if the net will appear. And living for the next upswing of a high that will catch her just in time.

My days have always been defined as good or bad by the latest good thing that has happened to me.

One night a few months ago, a storm blew in over the water where our house sits on the Long Island Sound. It came out of nowhere and quickly turned into one of the worst gales we've ever seen. Or rather *didn't* see. And that was the problem. We could hear the winds howling and the waves crashing against the seawall, a twelve-foot stone barrier that is the only thing standing between us and the certain

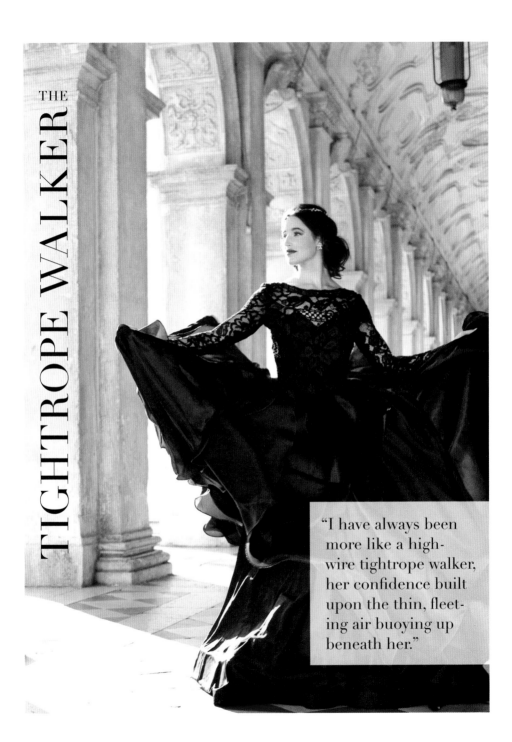

THE TIGHTROPE WALKER

"I have always been more like a high-wire tightrope walker, her confidence built upon the thin, fleeting air buoying up beneath her."

disaster of our house and everything we love in it being swallowed up whole. But even though we heard it clear as day, in the darkness our eyes could only make out the crest of sea spray as it breached the wall, lit only by the spotlight from a lone streetlamp. Minutes that felt like hours wore on as the waves continued to batter mercilessly against the wall. The waters rose so high and crashed so hard, their brutal castoff landing salty and stinging against our windows, pelting the double-pane glass some thirty feet away. It was the only time in ten years of living here that we were genuinely terrified of the Sound, afraid that this time it might actually breach the wall.

And we realized that there in the darkness, we would never know it was happening until it was too late.

I prayed loud to God that night. Petitioning him to put a protective hand upon our house, to speak but a word and calm the storm. I prayed bold prayers in faith and with a holy-fire confidence that I don't often see from myself.

Most times when the storms of life rage, I am far more like that doubter in the surging sea, driven and tossed by the winds of change. I am the *ye*, as in "O ye of little faith." I am Peter, stepping out of my comfort zone so that I can one day tell the story of the waves I've walked. Until I look down at my own feet, look down at my own circumstances, and at once . . . I am sinking. Drowning in a sea—or a mere six inches—of my own doubts and disbelief. I am one of the disciples—the very ones who have already witnessed the miracles Jesus can perform, have seen them with their own eyes—who suddenly find themselves back in that same old boat of still fearing the storm.

When we tether our lives and our very worth to our achieving, we become like that high-wire aerialist—our confidence constantly rising and falling, forever walking a tightrope between winning and losing, between praise on the world's lips and the inevitable criticism that

> *WHEN WE TETHER OUR LIVES AND OUR VERY WORTH TO OUR ACHIEVING, WE BECOME LIKE THAT HIGH-WIRE AERIALIST.*

comes and knocks the wind right out of us. Crashing with each new wave. Sure, there is a certain thrill to flying. But when the bottom falls out, make no mistake: it lands with a thud.

Up until now, my days have always been defined as good or bad by the latest good thing that has happened to me.

But I'm learning it is in those moments when we aren't sure if the safety net will appear in time or the protective barrier will hold, this is when our faith is forged in the storm.

The Bible tells us that Jesus "awoke and rebuked the wind and said to the sea, 'Peace! Be still!' And the wind ceased, and there was a great calm" (Mark 4:39).

Are we putting our tossed and tumbled hope in this high-wire act of waiting for the next good thing to happen to us? Or are we day by day putting our rock-solid, unshakable faith in the One who can silence the storm with a word?

GOD,

I thank you for all the ways you are still walking on water. I thank you for a hand extended to me over the waves. You are not just offering me a lifeline in the midst of drowning. You are inviting me to rise above and walk with you on the seas.

Thank you for your unwavering patience with me when I begin to sink in the depths of my own doubt. Thank you for your kind and loving face leaning down close to me and whispering, "It is I. Do not be afraid."

Forgive me for every time I am tempted to let go of your hand and leap without you, believing it is the only way I can fly.

I choose you, God.

I choose to build my life on the rock-solid ground that is trusting in you. In you I am unshakable. I am unafraid.

Let the wind howl.

Let the storms rage.

You are the rock wall that will not be moved.

AMEN.

SLOW GROWTH PRAYER

if you want character, you have to deal with what came before

3

HONOR THE FOUNDATION ON WHICH WE STAND

*And the rain fell, and
the floods came, and
the winds blew and beat
on that house, but it did
not fall, because it had
been founded on the rock.*

MATTHEW 7:25

WE LIVE IN a little 1880s fixer-upper by the sea.

For ten years, my husband Justin and I have been re-making this home in our own image, walking that thin, threaded line of giving new life to this house while also giving honor to the history that came before. We have these off-white linen curtains in our second-floor living room. In the early days of summer, when the air has not yet gone thick with humidity, we'll throw open all the windows and the door to our upstairs porch. And cool salt air will make billowing parachutes out of the curtains, these North Atlantic currents of linen cloth sails buoying up to float all around us that never seem to land.

A house needs air to breathe.

The walls are crooked in an old house. It's like the builders back then couldn't be bothered with something so puritan or pedestrian as a level . . . or a measuring tape.

This past summer we tried putting in built-in bookshelves as part of our living room renovation. When the shelves were in and the brackets were fastened and the last remaining molding was set to be installed—you can't make this up—the last board across the top had to be cut down three inches shorter on one side. Because that's how much the ceiling drops down.

Sometimes I think about how much easier it would be to live in a new construction. To make our home among a place that was built from the ground up just for us, entirely brand-new. It would be designed for the life we have now. Every wall straight as an arrow, the kitchen cabinets all shiny and soft-closing. We wouldn't have to deal with the slamming doors. We wouldn't have to deal with the ruins and the rubble. We wouldn't have to build upon the mistakes somebody else made.

It's hard building a life when you are constantly dealing with what came before, when there is history there. These generational patterns you feel called to break. Entire chapters that had nothing to do with you, and yet they haunt these hallways. I feel like easy-story people get these blank slates, this fresh new construction untouched by the past. They get to move in, hang a Magnolia wreath on the door, and call it done.

Hard-story people, on the other hand, are left to build where others left off. To fix what can be fixed. To honor the foundation on which they stand. And to try to leave it all a little better than they found it.

In a house—and in life—shiny and brand-new will always be easier.

But if you want *character*, you're going to have to deal with what came before.

THE

PERFORMER

"And so she succeeds almost compulsively in this urgent attempt to outrun failure. She believes all this achieving is the penance she has to pay for taking up space, the price of admission to be in most rooms."

AN A-PLUS is worth five dollars.

The first time I ever realized that there was an actual, literal worth that could be attached to my achieving, I was seven years old and entering the first nine weeks of second grade. That was when we struck our deal. Mom and Dad had seen firsthand that I was capable of getting straight A's from my time in kindergarten and first grade. So, to keep that streak alive, they decided to employ some good old-fashioned capitalism and a dose of meritocracy with a side of trading in futures to negotiate with me on my upcoming performance.

The sliding scale went something like this. For any of my seven subjects where I got an A-plus they would give me five dollars. An A would fetch a comparable though slightly less desirable $4.50. An A-minus quickly brought me down to a round, even four dollars, and I just as quickly learned how much the margins could cost you in this life. I became a person who always wanted *more*.

Once we entered B territory, the numbers dropped off steeply. And by the time we were in the C-plus range, an inverse scale kicked in and I had to start paying them. The message was loud and clear, at least as my seven-year-old ears heard it: there is a *cost* to being average.

It was wildly effective.

I think the little entrepreneur in me also came alive that day. And I quickly set about planning how I would reinvest every last penny of the $35 my seven subjects would surely fetch. Because right there in that moment, I had already decided how the rest of my life would go.

99

THE MESSAGE WAS LOUD AND CLEAR: THERE IS A COST TO BEING AVERAGE.

From that day forward, at least in my eyes, anything less than an A-plus performance would be considered nothing short of an abject failure.

WHEN YOU WALK into any room, she is probably the most put-together person in it.

Whether she's leading or speaking, making people feel welcome and seen, being the social butterfly, the capable one, the one people turn to for answers, or the best-dressed one there—the point is, you would never know only by looking at her the hard things she has had to overcome in her life.

That's because she has spent a lifetime running away from her muddy story.

Make no mistake. The Most Put-Together Woman in the Room never gets that way because that's how she *feels*. She feels like at any moment she will be found out. A fraud. A walking, waking imposter.

She doesn't do it to make anyone else feel small either. She walks in without a hair out of place, always delivering an A-plus performance at whatever she does, because she has convinced herself that this is the *bare minimum standard* she has to hit just to be welcome in most rooms. Just to be invited to have a seat at most tables.

And still she walks into any room and feels like it—like *she*—will never be enough. She could swear that the smell of mildew and dollar-store vanilla perfume still precedes her wherever she goes, introducing her before she can even say a word. She feels like every one of her scars is still burning on display, despite her best designer attempts to cover them up. She thinks everyone she meets can see right through her.

And so she succeeds almost compulsively in this urgent attempt to outrun failure. She believes all this achieving is the penance she has to pay for taking up space, the price of admission to be in most rooms.

All the while Fear sits upon her shoulders and hisses in her ears that none of it will have ever been enough. So day by day she builds empires out of the rubble and the ruins. She clutches her pearls and puts on the uniform and mask of a woman who has never once doubted that she belongs.

She succeeds despite (and to spite) her own story.

But what she doesn't realize is that those scars she bears are actually her superpower. They have made her stronger, kinder, more empathetic, more resilient than she'll ever know. And if she thinks that up until this point she's had an impact, just wait until she finds a way to *own* her own story.

I have spent way too much of my life being The Most Put-Together Woman in the Room. And what I've realized is that I have a lot more in common with that old 1880s fixer-upper than I thought. We both need salt air to breathe. We are both trying to honor and also correct for the history that came before. The history that still haunts these hallways. We have more value than anyone ever initially gives us credit for. And it is because of what we are made of that we are still standing here today. The rain fell and the floods came, but we did not fall. Because we are founded on the rock.

It's time to lead and love from that place.

Because in life, shiny and brand-new will no doubt always be easier.

But if we want the world to see our *character*, sooner or later we're going to have to deal with what came before.

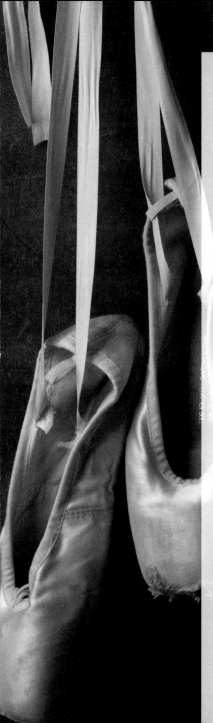

GOD,

You are the firm foundation on which we stand.

Thank you for how you are daily reminding us that what matters most is not the ease of our stories but the character of what is being built.

Thank you for the integrity and the care with which you have raised us up. You have made it possible that the bad stuff never truly got into the construction of our hearts.

I praise you for the freedom that is already available to us, the permission to finally lay down these versions of ourselves we once thought we had to become in order to belong.

Give us the courage to show up in vulnerability, God.

Help us to stop white-knuckling perfection and to lead from a place of love and authenticity.

Remind us that when we show up just as we are, just as you created us, it gives others the courage and permission to do the same.

AMEN.

SLOW GROWTH PRAYER

we have to stop living our whole life to please other people who spend their whole life

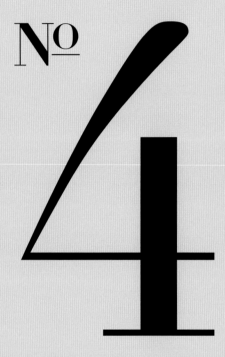

№ 4

ON FILTERS AND
UNDERDOG MOVIES

Now we see in a mirror dimly, but then face to face. Now I know in part; then I shall know fully, even as I have been fully known.

1 CORINTHIANS 13:12

DO YOU WANT TO KNOW the first face I picture when something really good happens to me?

It's not the faces of my parents, if that's what you're thinking, a wistful "Oh, won't they be so proud of me" expression flooding across my features. It's not the face of my husband either, or of my closest friends. It's not my business coach, my team, my friends twice removed on Facebook, or even the furry faces of my very fluffy dogs.

It is also *not* the face of God that I see first, this image of him that I hold in my mind of a gentle, warm, glowing light radiating out a "well done faithful servant" stare. A silent utterance of express approval shining down from the ether and lighting up a procession of cotton candy clouds on the horizon with these "God loves the earth" magnificent rays.

No, it's none of those.

This is where we know you and I *must* be really deep now in this business of being honest and transparent with one another.

Because the real, honest—I wish I could take it back every time, the very second it happens—answer is that it is a series of faces that flash through my mind of every single person who has ever told me that I *can't*. It is every person who has ever underestimated me, counted me out, discounted what I was capable of, or left me out on purpose when they were making up the invitations.

It's every person who has ever made me feel like the underdog in some 1980s John Hughes movie, simply by making it clear that I can't sit with them at the popular table. I'm Molly Ringwald in a home-made pink polka-dot prom dress standing by herself at the dance. Or Molly Ringwald when everybody forgets her birthday and she's . . . standing by herself at the dance. But definitely not Molly Ringwald as the homecoming queen in detention—these are very important distinctions we need to make.

Maybe that's a problem with growing up in the eighties. Most of those movies have given me a filter for how I look at life, one where the underdog is always the real star of the show. This filter says that everyone has to start out being against you, has to discount you for 95 percent of the plot if you are ultimately ever going to get everything you ever wanted in those last few minutes before the credits roll. You want your tabletop moment where you get to have your Jake and eat your cake too? Fine. But people are going to have to not even know you exist for most of your movie.

I heard this quote recently on a TV show—I can't remember which one, but it was probably from some really deep and philosophical character like Johnny Lawrence on *Cobra Kai*—and I can't stop thinking about it:

"Is she intimidating? Or are you *intimidated*?"

In other words, is this something the other person is actually doing to you? Are they actively trying to make you feel small? Or is it only something you assume is happening all around you because of how you feel on the inside?

Whether we realize it or not, every one of us is walking around with a filter (when I picture this, here I like to imagine those trifocal Benjamin Franklin glasses Nic Cage wears in *National Treasure*) we look through that shows us how we see the world. Or maybe, more to the point, it is a filter that shows us how we believe *the world sees us*.

Mine just so happens to tell me that I am the one people will always underestimate, the one people will always leave out.

In every sea of faces taking part in awkward cocktail party chitchat, I will always be the last one anyone would ever pick to go on to do big things. There are always people there who are louder, who have more followers, who have more names they can drop, who always seem like the *very important people* to go rub elbows with. Meanwhile, I will always be the person you'll find off in some dark corner somewhere hanging out with only one other person while we discuss our deepest hopes and fears.

"Hi, I just met you. What hidden shame are you carrying around that we can work on tonight?" I'm *super* fun at parties, guys.

There are, of course, times when the filter has been true—when I was left out, when someone did discount my worth. But there have been plenty more places in my story where this has not been true. Those times when I *was* picked first for the team. When the crazy good opportunity *did* land in my lap. When people saw something good in me that I could not see in myself and called me up to that place. When the doors swung open. When the voice that was speaking from the stage was my own.

But my filter does not like me to spend too much time thinking about those moments. Because every time I do, the filter becomes a little more transparent. Like Marty McFly's family disappearing from the four corners of a photograph, my filter knows that if it's going to survive, it can't allow me to change too much of the story. At least the one I've been telling myself in my head.

So my filter becomes an expert game maker dealing in a currency of confirmation bias. *Whatever I look for, I find.* Every rejection, every "not yet," every closed door, every group of people hanging out without me—they all become fodder for the filter that loves to keep me convinced the whole world is against me. That the whole world is getting together somewhere to have secret meetings, everyone taking bets and rooting for me to fail.

So when something good *does* happen, all I can think of are the people who just got proven wrong. The people who are going to have to stand off on the sidelines with their big-hair bangs and that 1980s mean-girl look on their faces, watching while Molly Ringwald finally gets asked to dance. And yet in doing that, I'm inviting those very same people (real or imagined) to become the *first* people who get access to me when the time comes to celebrate. They become unintended front-row guests to all my best moments in life.

While I'm at it, I guess I do the very same thing when something *bad* happens too.

> **WHETHER WE REALIZE IT OR NOT, EVERY ONE OF US IS WALKING AROUND WITH A FILTER FOR HOW WE BELIEVE THE WORLD SEES US.**

When the outcome is disappointing. When my name doesn't get called. When things are taking much longer than I had hoped. These are the faces I fill the front row with then too. I let them pull up a chair and scoot in nice and close all around me, their faces nearly pressed up against mine. I let them sneer at my setbacks and "told you so" all over my disappointments. The schadenfreude is practically palpable; you can feel it in the air.

When we give people (real or imagined) who aren't *for* us a front-row seat to our lives, our happy times are cut in half and our sorrows are doubled by the mere scrutiny of their presence.

We have to stop doing that.

The day you realize you've turned your entire life into a 1980s underdog movie is the day you start to rewrite the script. The day you realize that things are not always as they seem but have been colored and distorted by the filter you see the world through is the day you start to see clearly.

But the day you realize that the *only* filter that matters is the way that God sees you—this crystal-clear reflection of the "you" you are becoming—*that* is the day you start to become free.

Real or imagined, how other people see us does not ultimately matter.

So we have to stop living as if our entire lives revolve around proving them wrong.

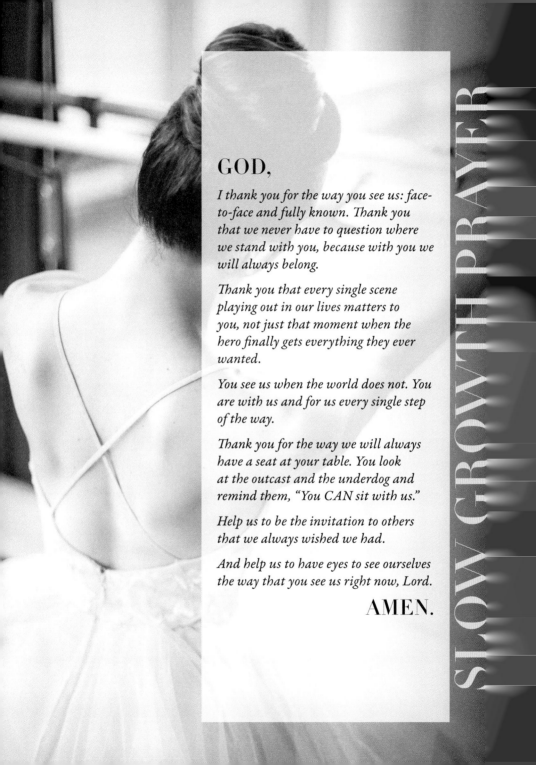

GOD,

I thank you for the way you see us: face-to-face and fully known. Thank you that we never have to question where we stand with you, because with you we will always belong.

Thank you that every single scene playing out in our lives matters to you, not just that moment when the hero finally gets everything they ever wanted.

You see us when the world does not. You are with us and for us every single step of the way.

Thank you for the way we will always have a seat at your table. You look at the outcast and the underdog and remind them, "You CAN sit with us."

Help us to be the invitation to others that we always wished we had.

And help us to have eyes to see ourselves the way that you see us right now, Lord.

AMEN.

No 5

take a deep breath and ask: what does success actually look like to me?

THE CHECKLIST OF OTHER PEOPLE'S SUCCESS

For they loved the glory that comes from man more than the glory that comes from God.

IF YOU AND I are going to give up achieving for our worth, then we are also going to have to give up other people's opinions of our lives.

I know that statement should be obvious. Apparent. A truth we hold to be self-evident. I *know* that.

But the first time that thought flashed through my mind it was like a wild animal that fixes its cold, calculating eyes on you from the edge of a deep, dark wood before disappearing in a streak—this dissipating chroma of color, a polaroid moving in reverse. The first time I was visited by that untamed thought, it was groundbreaking to me. A revelation. Something even approaching *epiphany* status.

Let me show you what I mean.

Imagine that for the next ten years you will live life inside the confines of a small, white cube. It is a blank slate. An empty square waiting for you to fill it with what matters. During this time, you are free to go after and achieve any goal you set your mind to. You are free to accumulate and acquire, earn, spend, and outperform. The only thing you *can't* do is tell anybody about it.

In something approaching a tree falling in the woods when there's no one there to hear it, does a highlight reel without an audience even make a sound?

In other words, when we achieve for our worth, we are implicitly relying on other people being there to see it . . . and somehow deem it *worthy*. In doing that, we hand over all the power in our own lives to people who may not ever deserve it.

When I look at my own life, this becomes both a litmus test and a way forward.

Which brings me to my second revelation: If you and I are going to give up achieving for our worth, then we are *also* going to have to give up other people's versions of success.

Here's why.

It's so easy to look around and see all of the amazing things other people are doing and start to assign their successes an empty box on your own checklist. Like a blank space in your life or a blinking cursor in your own story, it becomes one more step between where you are and where you *think* you have to be in order to call yourself successful. It starts to go a little something like this.

We see a friend or a stranger on the internet do A—let's say start a new business. Then we see some other person we know do B—maybe start building their dream house. Then we see that person we've looked up to for years post about doing C—perhaps it's taking that dream vacation we've always wanted to go on or getting a brand-new

kitchen that looks like it could have been ripped directly from our "Kitchen Dreaming" Pinterest board.

And then our brain does this really tricky sleight of hand.

Even though we saw one person do A, another person do B, and still another person do C . . . somewhere in our heads it becomes, "Okay, so in order to be successful I must do all three: A, B and C." In other words, we build up those three separate mere mortals in our own minds and assemble them into some sort of greater-than-the-sum-of-their-parts Transformer—this Decepticon of success that *none* of us could ever live up to. Because we're giving each of them credit for three things when in reality they have each done only one.

And we don't stop at A, B, and C either. We keep adding, heaping onto the list, until we make it all the way to Z and have ourselves convinced that the *only* way we can be successful is if we tie ourselves up in knots trying to juggle all twenty-six of these things at once.

We tell ourselves that we're not really successful unless we're globe-trotting Europe *while* dressing like a J.Crew ad *while* redecorating our magazine-worthy and super clean home *while* writing amazing blog posts that go viral *while* growing a super huge Instagram following *while* spending quality time with our friends *while* being the perfect wife and mother *while* . . . the list goes on and on.

> "
> *BEFORE I ADD YET ANOTHER CHECK MARK TO AN ALREADY OVERSTUFFED LIST, I ASK MYSELF: AM I DOING IT FOR ME . . . OR AM I DOING IT FOR THEM?*

And it's *exhausting*.

It's exhausting just reading that list. But here's the really scary part . . . that's how we're living our whole life. We're living for the checklist of somebody else's success. And the truth is, we're setting ourselves up for failure because we're starting with a list that no human is actually accomplishing. It's just a greatest-hits compilation we've curated in our own head and we're giving everyone else credit for.

So here's my litmus test moving forward.

Before I add yet another check mark to an already overstuffed list of all the things I hope to one day aspire to, I ask myself: Am I doing it for me . . . or am I doing it for *them*?

Am I doing it because I feel like it fulfills a purpose and a calling over my life? Am I doing it because I feel like God is asking me to and I want to be obedient? Or am I doing it in the hopes that this time— *this time*—it will finally make me enough of something to sit at those same tables where no one could be bothered to scoot down and make room for me in the first place?

Let's stop doing it for them.

Let's stop putting our worth in the hands of people who can't be bothered to notice . . . or who notice everything but pretend they don't see it in order to make us feel small. In either case, if we are going to get healthy, if we are going to get free of this addiction to achieving, we cannot do it by allowing other people's version of success to dictate our own.

Today, I want you to recognize your success meter for what it might actually be: the checklist of somebody else's dream. Take a deep breath and ask yourself . . . what does success *actually* look like for me?

Now let's go do that.

SLOW GROWTH PRAYER

GOD,

Thank you that you have a plan for our lives that has absolutely nothing to do with people-pleasing or attempting to earn our worth in other people's eyes.

Thank you that the list you have for us is actually pretty simple: love God and love other people.

Help us to see exactly how empty these very full lists of ours have become.

Open our eyes to the fact that most things in this world are not as they seem. And there is no checklist or (blue) check mark that can ever make us any more worthy of love.

Help us to let go of what everyone else is chasing.

And help us, God, to look to one place and one place only for what our next step should be: you, Lord.

AMEN.

№ 6

we have to be willing to let go of other people's plans for our lives

A PENSKE TRUCK'S WORTH OF EXPECTATIONS

In him we have obtained an inheritance,
having been predestined according to
the purpose of him who works all things
according to the counsel of his will.

EPHESIANS 1:11

MY GRANDMA GOLDIE'S youngest sister—the youngest born in a long line of thirteen—was a woman named Charlotte Ann, which would technically make her my great-aunt Charlotte. But to me she was always just Aunt Annie.

She had fire-red, short, curly hair—which, as the years wore on, I suspect only stayed that way thanks in part to the contribution of Revlon—and a fiery, red-hot personality to go with it. She was barely five foot tall, practically lived in Goodwill T-shirts and brand-new Nikes, and zipped around town in a navy blue Ford Escort that she always affectionately called Bessie.

There was a pronounced bump in the bridge of her nose, knocked crooked some years earlier by a husband who knew how to nurse a bottle and land a punch. She had sent him packing years before I was born. And instead chose to raise her two boys on her own as a single parent living in one of the poorer parts of Akron, Ohio, with only a meager income working the lunch line of what she always called "the old folks home" to support them.

It turns out *one part firecracker, one part sassafras* is something that runs in our family.

Annie didn't get along with a lot of people. And a *lot* of people didn't get along with Annie. But when I was really little she taught me how to remember the extra-long name of her hometown newspaper, the *Akron Beacon Journal Times Press*, by having me tap a circle around my face starting with my forehead, cheek, chin, and then the other cheek, before finally landing on my nose for "Press."

I thought that was the funniest thing. And from that moment on, Aunt Annie loved me like I was her own.

Annie was known for being a hard worker. Goldie always said she worked circles around all the other employees at the nursing home. Which, when I was little, made me wonder how she ever got anything done if she was always running around in circles like that. But Goldie seemed to know what she was talking about, so I just shrugged my shoulders and agreed.

I was twenty-five when my fiery, active, hard-working, great Aunt Annie took a slip and fall at work. She hit her head. And before we knew what was happening, she was in a nursing home herself. And then just like that, she was gone.

Shortly after that, I got a call from an insurance lady saying that Annie had named me as a beneficiary to her life insurance and that there was also a storage unit in Akron with my name on it. Annie had always told me that she was keeping a hope chest for me for one day when I got married. So my then-fiancé, Justin, and I drove from Connecticut to Ohio in my cherry-red Neon.

To see what all Annie had *hoped* for my life.

"WE CAN'T SPEND OUR *whole* LIFE STORING UP THE *expectations* SOMEONE ELSE HAD FOR US."

WE ARE THE HEIRS TO DREAMS WE HAVE NEVER DREAMED. HOPES WE HAVE NEVER HOPED.

When it was all said and done, we ended up needing to rent the biggest truck Penske offered—the twenty-six footer—just to get it all home. Back in my driveway in the dead heat of summer, we unpacked the most motley crew of inventory we had ever seen. It ranged from expensive Tiffany crystal bowls she had found for cheap at yard sales in the "rich folks" neighborhoods to little angel ornaments from Goodwill, their creepy faces warped and melted from years of sitting in hot storage until they looked like they were crying little plastic tears. It took us weeks to get through all the boxes.

What to keep. What to let go of.

It's a strange thing to go through someone else's belongings after they have passed. A lifetime of accumulation, these unearthed artifacts that somehow make up an entire life bound up in dusty cardboard boxes. These things that once held so much importance, now left in limbo in the absence of the one who saw their value in the first place.

It's an even stranger thing to unpack an entire lifetime of dreams that someone else has held on your behalf.

Each and every one of us is walking around with a Penske truck's worth of dreams and expectations, hopes and sacrifices, possibilities and baggage that someone else has left us. We are the heirs to dreams we have never dreamed. Hopes we have never hoped. These crystal-plated versions of the so-called good life, a china pattern we never once picked out for ourselves.

We can spend a lifetime unpacking all that.

Where to go to school, what job to take, who to marry, where to live, how many kids to have, how much money is enough. These white-picket-fence wishes and keeping-up-with-the-Joneses dreams that were really just the hopes that somebody else had for *their* lives. Parents, grandparents, great-aunts twice removed. They are living vicariously through us, storing up a thousand of their own hoped-for happy moments that never once made their way out of the plastic. Until this version of a life we did not choose becomes our inheritance.

Let's be clear.

The people who want good things for us are filled with good intentions. The hopes they have for our lives are like a cup that runneth over, brimming with the prayer that one day we would have everything they never had. It can be beautiful. It can be sacrificial. And it can also be suffocating. Our job is to figure out what stays.

What to keep. What to let go of.

What we can't do is spend our whole life storing up the expectations someone else had for us, no matter how well intentioned. We can't go to our grave buried in the pile of what someone else thought would be good for us. The day we begin to find the answers is the day we start to edit our own version of the good life. It is the day we get into conversation with God about what he says matters, what he says lasts.

It's the day we go through a Penske truck's worth of *stuff* and realize we can't take any of it with us. That is when we begin to understand that the real legacy we'll pass down has always been a fighting spirit, an unbreakable work ethic, and loving others as our own.

One part firecracker, one part sassafras.

And that is a hope worth holding on to. ▮

SLOW GROWTH PRAYER

GOD,

Give us the courage to chart our own path, looking to you for the directions.

Help us to honor every sacrifice made on our behalf without making little crystal-plated idols out of what someone else says is good for us, what someone else expects of our lives.

Help us to unpack what came before, to release what is no longer needed, and to honor the legacy that stays.

Help us to keep trusting in the purpose that you have for us, Lord, the inheritance you have already predestined.

Even when these steps don't make sense to human eyes, help us to keep trusting the muddy road you have laid out before us.

And the hope we have in you alone.

AMEN.

it's time to lay down these heavy things

A BOULDER ROLLING DOWN THE MOUNTAIN

Come to me, all you who are weary and burdened, and I will give you rest. Take my yoke upon you and learn from me, for I am gentle and humble in heart, and you will find rest for your souls. For my yoke is easy and my burden is light.

MATTHEW 11:28–30 NIV

FOR FAR TOO LONG IN MY LIFE, I imagined my days were like one big exercise in Sisyphus and his elusive rock.

If you aren't up on your obscure Greek mythology references, let me catch you up to speed here. Sisyphus was a guy who, because of his own ancient version of humblebrags and highlight reels, irritated Zeus just enough to get himself sentenced to an eternity of rolling a huge boulder up a hill over and over, only for it to roll all the way back down every time it neared the top.

That was how I saw every goal I was chasing.

I have spent years feeling like I couldn't let go for a second—couldn't pause to rest, didn't dare stop pushing—for fear that the whole thing would go tumbling back to the bottom and I would be forced to start over from the beginning. In my world, there was no room for plateaus. No scenic mountain overlooks. No wide places in the road to pull over and rest for a little while along the journey. Unpack a picnic. Maybe read some Shakespeare.

There was only pushing and climbing. Goal setting and grinding. I was forever neck-deep in the hustle and breaking my own back. Never stopping. Never breathing. I kept my eyes on the prize, not even blinking for a second until I reached the top lest the whole thing come crashing down around me.

Progress was a dirty word in the face of my vocabulary rooted only in perfection. I didn't want grace. I didn't want a participation trophy. I wanted nothing short of the mountaintop moment. And it was going to be *my* pushing, *my* effort alone that got me there.

In case it isn't clear, *this is not biblical.*

Jesus never said, "Come to me all you who are weary and burdened, and I will give you a giant boulder to push up a hill over and over until you die." He said, "Come to me and I will give you rest."

Rest.

Rest has also been a dirty word in my life's vocabulary for far too long. It's as if I was born to push. As if it's wired in me right down to my DNA.

Our friends have one of those Samoyed dogs—basically a super fluffy, white husky—and one of the things they learned very quickly is that if they don't give this animal *work* to do, he will turn destructive. He will tear the house down to the studs with all his pent-up anxious energy. He was born to be a sled dog, to pull and pull and forever plow his way forward. Dragging people behind him when he has to. It's like he was born with an unlimited supply of productivity, and if he doesn't find something to do *daily* with all this energy . . . he will destroy everything in his path.

I am the same kind of animal.

I am like a sled dog. Or one of those oxen that were always wandering off in *Oregon Trail*, looking for work to do when they were meant to be resting, thereby making you lose two extra days in the process. On top of getting dysentery.

When it comes to rest, I'm basically like a big, dumb animal who doesn't know any better. A beast of burden. All I can ever think is, *If I stop to rest, what will become of my boulder?* Never once realizing that somewhere along the way I have become a prisoner to carrying very heavy things. It's like I'm more concerned about the punishment of pushing than I am the freedom that is offered in rest.

I am driven by purpose. And meaning. And doing things that make me feel like I matter. I am wired to set goals and then push and push until I hit them, forever plowing my way forward to some unnamed, unseen destination in the distance. Dragging everyone else around behind me, kicking and screaming, when I have to. But pushing forward nonetheless.

Removing this work of achieving for my worth is like asking a sled dog to nap all day. It goes against my very nature. And in the absence of some other satisfying work to do, it will eventually be my undoing.

The minute we decide to give up all this achieving for our worth, an inevitable silence settles in. A vacuum in the shape of a black hole immediately sucks all the air out of the room—this very same place where the once overstuffed, overscheduled, overmanaged life mockery

> **IF I STOP TO REST, WHAT WILL BECOME OF MY BOULDER?**

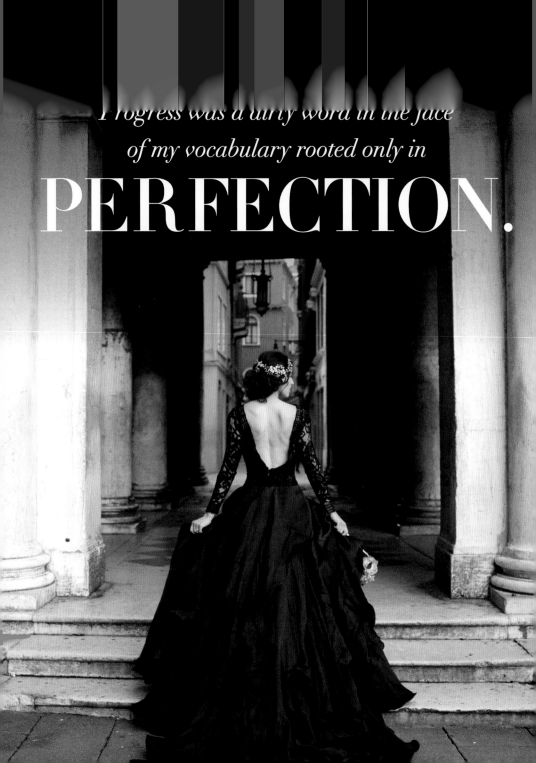

Progress was a dirty word in the face of my vocabulary rooted only in

PERFECTION.

of our own making used to reside. Now, in the midst of the darkness settled in, it is the absence of something that does all the shouting.

Put simply: *Now what?*

What are we supposed to do with the rest of our life if this endless pursuit of gold stars and check marks is no longer on the table? Who even *are* we without the latest post highlighting our newest accomplishment? If we go too long without the world knowing we've done something worthy, will we just cease to exist altogether?

And I think Jesus gets that about us.

There is a reason he also says, "For my yoke is easy, and my burden is light."

I think it's so beautiful that Jesus would use the imagery of a yoke—something that was typically used to subject animals to the bondage of constantly plowing forward, driven ever onward by the heavy weight they carried on their shoulders—to represent the true freedom that is only found in coming to him for rest. He's saying you can lay down the weight of the hustle, this constant spinning and striving, trying to work your way into worth.

But if we look closer, there is something else there. I once read a devotional from Shaunti Feldhahn where she talked about how a yoke for work animals has to be measured very specifically. If it's off even a little bit, it can end up making the animal have to work twice as hard for the same result.* This is what happens when we try to accomplish our work apart from God. There is a reason a yoke is fashioned with two openings, to tether our own efforts to another's. When the yoke we take on is one that has been custom made for us, and when the other half of that yoke is one that has us harnessed directly to Jesus, it is only then that our burden becomes light. There is no more pushing, no pulling, no rolling the boulder back up the hill. There is only the

---

*Shaunti Feldhahn, *Find Rest: A Women's Devotional for Lasting Peace in a Busy Life* (Alpharetta, GA: iDisciple, 2018), 7.

work that was created uniquely for us. And a source of strength we could never have on our own.

That is when we can have maximum impact.

Resting to sit at the feet of Jesus doesn't mean our boulder will roll back down the hill. It is a wide-open overlook along the journey. It allows us to pause and take in the view. Appreciate the climb. Maybe even play a Miley Cyrus song. And it means that when we are ready to go back and do the work that God has called us to, our efforts won't be in vain.

Let us never believe that time spent with God is wasted or means sacrificing our goals. Spending time with God tells us where to put our efforts, when to push and when to rest. It is the very difference between starting over and gaining spacious ground.

It's time to lay down these heavy things.

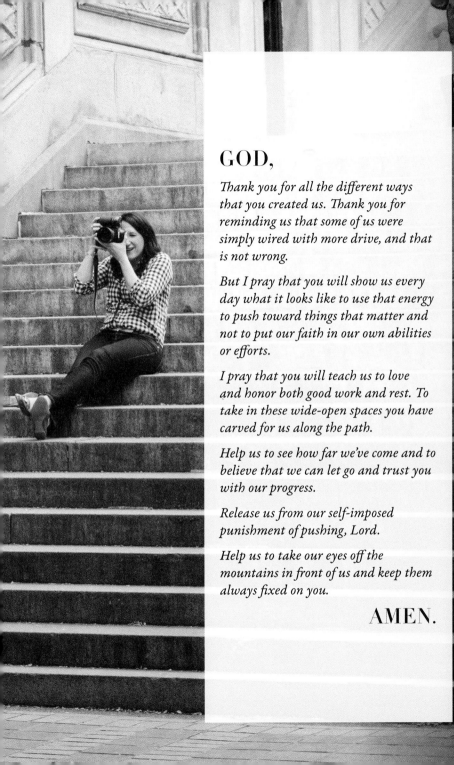

GOD,

Thank you for all the different ways that you created us. Thank you for reminding us that some of us were simply wired with more drive, and that is not wrong.

But I pray that you will show us every day what it looks like to use that energy to push toward things that matter and not to put our faith in our own abilities or efforts.

I pray that you will teach us to love and honor both good work and rest. To take in these wide-open spaces you have carved for us along the path.

Help us to see how far we've come and to believe that we can let go and trust you with our progress.

Release us from our self-imposed punishment of pushing, Lord.

Help us to take our eyes off the mountains in front of us and keep them always fixed on you.

AMEN.

you can spend your whole life chasing crumbs, but freedom is in the other direction

№ 8

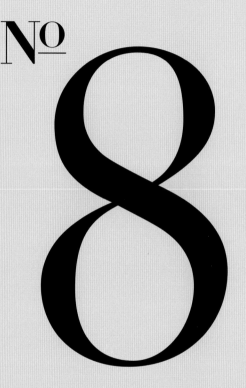

FRENETIC,
FRENZIED, FRANTIC

It is in vain that you rise up early and go late to rest, eating the bread of anxious toil; for he gives to his beloved sleep.

PSALM 127:2

THE SEPTEMBER AFTER I graduated law school at Yale—when Justin and I made the decision to turn down not one but two six-figure law firm offers in London and New York to start a business together—we flew out to Los Angeles to attend our first ever photography conference.

After three days in a sterile, fluorescent-lit hotel ballroom, sitting in session after session and soaking up everything we could, we decided to rent a car and drive out into the desert rather than flying directly back home. We needed the windows rolled down, some wide-open stretches of highway out in front of us without another car in sight, the wild wind running its fingers through my hair as I rested my chin on my arm and watched the world blur by all around us.

There was a song on the radio from a blonde, curly-haired new country star singing all about Tim

McGraw. Justin held my hand, and we talked about the upcoming wedding we were planning and the family we would one day start. One boy, one girl. We were on the horizon of the rest of our lives, literally driving off into the sunset. And it felt like there was *nothing* we couldn't do.

About thirty miles outside of Las Vegas sits a blue-green, man-made body of water known as Lake Mead. We pulled the car off the second we saw it, an oasis in the middle of a vast, dry land. We got out and let the sun fall warm on our faces, the bright light blinding as it glinted off the white sandstone quarry of rock all around us. We needed to stretch our legs.

But what happened was about to stretch our perspective for years to come.

At the end of a short pathway, the sidewalk gave way to floating dock. And suddenly on either side of our feet the water was churning and alive with a thousand gulping gray fish just gasping to survive. Their round, hungry mouths shouting at us to feed them more of what they need, screaming out at us above all the noise without ever once making a sound. They are part of the on-site hatchery there at the lake, which is intended to be educational. And that day they *were* about to give us an education—but probably not in the way that was expected.

As we stood there watching those fish—frenetically thrashing and flopping all over one another, trying to be the one who came out on top even if it meant pushing another one under—all I could think was, here are all of these wild things fighting it out in captivity over mere *crumbs* when there is a whole wide expanse of freedom if they would only turn around and swim the other direction.

The word *frenetic* is derived from the same root as *frenzied* and *frantic*. But it also makes me think of that word *frequency*, which in science terms can be used to describe vibrational energy between

TURN
AROUND.

Freedom is in the other direction.

atoms in a molecule. Atoms exert massive opposing vibrations in this constant push-pull effect just to try to hold everything together. In other words, they exert *all* their energy . . . just to stay in one spot.

That's what we do too, isn't it? We waste all our energy running left and running right, trying to keep up with what everyone else is doing, without it ever once moving us forward. We flop all over ourselves, trying to get ahead, trying to hold it all together, trying to get more, fighting it out in captivity just to get our share of the crumbs. Never once realizing that freedom is at our backs.

For years after that, anytime Justin and I felt our business getting caught up in that comparison, in that scarcity, in that frenetic energy that made us feel like we were gasping for air just trying to survive, one of us would always take a deep breath and say to the other, "Lake Mead fish."

And we instantly knew that freedom was in the opposite direction.

One of the bravest things you'll ever do is to set out on your own and chart a brand-new course. To gaze off in the opposite direction from where everyone else is always running to so fast and allow yourself the quiet wonder of a solid, silent minute to go curiously and willfully wherever which way the wind draws you. Calls you. Beckons you home.

You can spend your whole life chasing currents. You can spend your whole life chasing trends. You can wish away your sails and long to be something faster. You can chug along, somehow always in last place in a race you never signed up for, wondering why you can never seem to pick up speed.

Or you can turn around, lift your determined face to the light, strike out boldly for a brand-new horizon. And realize that the second you are willing to turn away from what everyone else is chasing . . . that last place position suddenly puts you first in line for exactly what God has planned for you.

It's a big ocean. There is more than enough wind for everybody. And the most beautiful vessels, the kind people will remember? You'll know them when you see them out there doing exactly what they were created to do.

Two days after our stop at Lake Mead, Justin and I sat and watched the sun come up over the Grand Canyon. We found a ledge where we weren't afraid of falling, and we held on to one another as the light cast a thousand ruddy rainbows against a painted sky. I sat there in the great expanse, and finally it felt like we had found enough wide-open space where I could breathe again.

Aren't you *tired* of being frenetic, frenzied, and frantic?

Turn around. Freedom is in the other direction.

GOD,

I thank you that you are a God of peace.

In the work you are calling me to, I always know when I have moved from a place of purpose to a place of striving and self-reliance by checking in to see if my heart is racing.

If I feel frenetic.

If it feels like I have to hurry up and get my piece of the pie before someone else takes everything.

God, I know you do not operate out of a scarcity currency.

You are not in a rush.

You are not in a hurry.

Help me to remember that if I find myself exerting all of this energy just to stay in one spot, chances are . . . freedom is behind me.

Help me to turn around and cast my eyes back on you.

AMEN.

N<u>o</u>

9

I'LL BE HAPPY
WHEN . . .

comparison is a moving target—the next big thing is always just out of reach

I have learned the secret of being content in any and every situation, whether well fed or hungry, whether living in plenty or in want. I can do all this through him who gives me strength.

PHILIPPIANS 4:12 NIV

WE HAVE SPENT a heartbreaking amount of our lives believing the lie "I'll be happy when . . ."

When I finish school.

When the bills are all caught up.

When the debt is paid off.

When we buy our first house.

When I finally find someone to love.

I'll be happy *when* I get that recognition. I'll be happy *when* I achieve that goal. I'll be happy *when* I'm making that much money.

I'll be happy when I am where *she* already is.

We've spent years thinking that happiness is barely beyond our fingertips—always just out of reach, always coming up around the next bend—a ship at sea still waiting to come in. It is a vanishing point barely beyond the grip of our horizon. We spend our lives in this posture of reaching, chasing future versions of ourselves we can never quite catch up to, only to finally wake up one day and realize the house of mirrors we were actually in. This distorted image of the good life, warped and ever-changing, has been tunneling our vision until we can no longer see clearly. And when the dust settles and our eyes are finally opened, the hard truth sets in.

All this running in circles only to find ourselves back at the beginning has cost us the one thing we can never get back: time.

Be honest. Close your eyes. How much of your life have you spent waiting to be happy *when*?

A flood of Decembers comes rushing into my mind. Stinging like icy, dark waters. Stark like a chorus of bare branches charcoal-sketched against the pale white of an ashen sky. A twinkle of lights strung together on evergreen branches the only warmth I can feel on my face. I have spent far too many Decembers looking back on the closing calendar behind me, a familiar sinking feeling of regret sitting heavy in my gut to remind me that yet another year is coming to a close and I still haven't gotten it right.

It was somewhere around the middle of December when I lay on the floor with my face buried in an old sweatshirt and cried angry, salty, stinging, bitter tears. They ran down my face without apology, and with each aerial bomb of a crashing drop I felt the weight on my shoulders growing heavier.

I was stuck. I was frustrated. I was furious at myself for not doing *more* . . . and being *more* . . . and having *more* to show for the year behind me that was so quickly fading away.

I was tired. Tired of watching somebody else chase every one of my dreams. Tired of watching other people do what I wanted to do and do it better. They were out there getting it done. Making each and every one of their dreams happen, like some golden to-do list that they were marching their way through like an invading army. And I was on the floor crying into an old sweatshirt.

I felt the impending downward spiral of the ugly, ugly comparison monster coming on, and in that moment I just let go and let it wash over me in waves. I told myself a flurry of lies about how that would never be me. I listed out all the things I would never be able to do, so what was the point in even trying. And I rocked the idea of giving up altogether back and forth in my crumpled hands as my sobs faded away into quiet tears.

It was not a pretty moment in my life.

I felt jealous, and angry at myself for being jealous. I felt lost, and angry at myself for being lost. I felt like a failure, and I was angry at myself for failing.

But somewhere in the smoldering ashes of just giving up altogether, a new spark started to take root.

THE COMEDY OF ERRORS in our lives is that we spend our days chasing the next high, believing that it is the very next hit of sugary-sweet achievement that will finally make us feel full. Which is an excellent way to spend your whole life hungry.

And perhaps the greatest cruelty of all is that after all of that buildup, it never feels how you think it's going to feel.

Think about when you were in middle school or junior high. Do you remember how grown-up, how *adult* the high school seniors looked to you back then? They had it all together. They could *drive*. They were about to leave home.

I remember thinking I knew exactly what it was going to feel like to be a senior. I remember thinking that if I could just get there, finally be on the verge of the rest of my own life, I was going to feel so different. And then you get there, you *arrive*, and it's not that it isn't great—there are so many exciting things that you are grateful for—but it just doesn't feel like what you *thought* it would.

Because by the time you get there, you already have your eyes on something new. Now you're looking to the people who are in college. Maybe the ones who are getting engaged or starting their first job or moving to a different state to chase some big dream. And you can't wait until you are where *they* are.

My point is, when you hit a goal it never *feels* quite the way you think it's going to feel, because by the time you hit that goal you have become an entirely different version of yourself than the one who first imagined it. And by then, you already have a whole new set of check marks you are chasing.

It's like a never-ending game of football where they keep moving the goal line on you, or like running a marathon where you find out the finish line is actually on the back of a flatbed truck driving all around the city. It's like a thousand-piece puzzle that actually turns out to be made up of ten-thousand parts.

In other words, it's a moving target.

And it *always* feels like there's another piece of the puzzle missing.

This is why achieving for our worth is an exercise in futility: it is both never enough and always just out of reach.

We have to stop chasing this imagined high of "I'll be happy when . . ." and we have to start falling in love with the hard, messy, beautiful, unfinished life that's right in front of us. In the here and now.

There will always be blanks in our lives waiting to be filled in.

In the meantime, let's get busy living out those first three words. *I'll be happy.*

GOD,

I am so thankful that in your infinite mercy you don't make me count up the minutes and hours, months and years of my life that I have already postponed LIVING . . . all while I was waiting for the next big thing to happen. I think that would actually break my heart, Lord, if I knew what that number really was.

I'm sorry for every second where I have acted like this exact life I have now is not miracle enough for me.

I'm sorry for comparing my life to someone else's. For wishing for their seemingly easy story or gold stars or to be where they are.

I have been chasing warped reflections of something always just up around the bend.

Meanwhile, you lean your face down close to mine in the here and now and gently whisper, "Look up. You're missing it."

Help me to open my eyes, God.

Help me to see every beautiful minute of it, this extraordinary life you have given me, while it's still mine to live.

AMEN.

SLOW GROWTH PRAYER

№

10

we get so focused on things that don't matter, that we're missing what does

THE CLOCK
IS TICKING

*O Lord, make me know my
end and what is the measure
of my days; let me know
how fleeting I am!*

PSALM 39:4

THERE IS THIS SCENE at the end of the play
Our Town where Emily, one of the lead characters, has
passed away and pauses to say goodbye before heading
to her grave. In one of the most remembered scenes in
theater history, she says:

> I can't go on. It goes so fast. We don't have time to
> look at one another. I didn't realize. So all that was
> going on and we never noticed. Take me back—up the
> hill—to my grave. But first: Wait! One more look.
>   Good-by, Good-by, world. Good-by, Grover's Cor-
> ners . . . Mama and Papa. Good-by to clocks ticking
> . . . and Mama's sunflowers. And food and coffee. And
> new-ironed dresses and hot baths . . . and sleeping and
> waking up. Oh, earth, you're too wonderful for any-
> body to realize you.*

*Thornton Wilder, *Our Town: A Play in Three Acts*, Act 3 (New York:
Harper & Row, 1938), 112.

The first time I ever read this, it broke my heart.

But the second time I read it, it opened my eyes.

You know what I don't see?

What I *don't* see is Emily saying, "Goodbye to bank accounts and thousands of followers, blue check marks and designer bags. Goodbye to my luxury SUV and that promotion at work and the vacation I can't wait to put on social media. Oh, Instagram, you're far too wonderful for anybody to realize you!"

I know, I know. Those things didn't exist in Grover's Corners. But something tells me that even if they did, they still wouldn't have made her list.

The stuff we think matters isn't going to be the stuff we miss.

I try to remind myself of this as often as I can.

I saw a post once that said something to the effect of, "The next time you're tempted to get frustrated at your husband for leaving his shoes in the middle of the floor, imagine that you lost him and how gently you would look at those shoes then." It's morbid, I know. But man, I have never been able to shake that. Every time I see a pair of Justin's shoes in the middle of the floor, or his dirty, punky socks tucked in between the couch and the coffee table, or a kitchen cabinet door standing wide open, I think about how much they would make me miss him if he were gone.

That's how it was a few years back when we lost Cooper, our golden retriever of twelve and a half years. What we noticed most that night when we came home from the emergency vet was how *quiet* the house was without him. We'd never noticed it before because he was a dog that we had heard bark maybe six times in his whole life. We had no idea how much the jingle-jangle of his collar and the *tap-tap-tap* of his paws coming around the corner on the hardwood floor had filled our home with so much love.

THE CLOCK

is ticking.

"WE HAD NO IDEA HOW MUCH THOSE *little* THINGS REALLY WERE THE *big* THINGS."

We had no idea how that tennis ball stuck under the couch, never to be chased again . . . or the blanket covered in the last of his fur . . . or the leash hanging from its usual place on the hook, just waiting to go on a walk with a golden fluffball who was never coming home again—we had *no idea* how much those little things really were the big things.

So I try not to forget that now.

Now I try to take in how extra soft the fur is on the ears of our two dogs, Goodspeed and Atticus. I try to really smell the coffee in the morning when I wake up and to feel the scruff of Justin's three-day-old beard against my cheek. I wiggle my toes against the cool cotton sheets and linen duvet and try to remind myself that these *are* the good old days.

Here's what I'm learning: success is not always going to look big and grand.

Sometimes it's going to look like having the kind of friend who shows up and sits with you on your best days . . . and on your hardest. Those moments when they say everything you need to hear without ever having to say a word. It's going to look like a phone call from your parent while you still have the chance to hear their voice on the other end of the line. It's a happy dance in the kitchen and soft pillows and a soft place to land. It's an unexpected card stuck in a book with just one more message from that person you would have given anything to have five more minutes with.

It's the sun pouring in through the window. A gentle salt breeze brushing your hair. The smell of garlic and fresh basil. And bare feet slow dancing on hardwood floors. It's the way you can feel a Van Morrison song all the way in the back of your throat—thick and slow and sweet like (Tupelo) honey. It's the perfect tomato from the garden with a little bit of salt. It's a front porch. And the perfect Sauv Blanc. It's two gigantic lap dogs to keep you warm when the air turns crisp in those first few days of fall. And a hand that has always fit perfectly in yours.

When my life is over and it's my turn to say goodbye, these will be the things I'll wish I had spent more time noticing. The things I'll wish I had more time for. Every one of a million, small, little, barely noticed, what's it matter, who's to say, out of the ordinary, un-ordinary nothings . . . that make up our whole lives together.

This mundane minutia that is nothing short of a miracle.

We get so focused on all those other things that we're *missing* it.

We're missing what's right in front of us. We aren't noticing it near enough. We aren't taking the time to really look at one another.

And the clock is ticking.

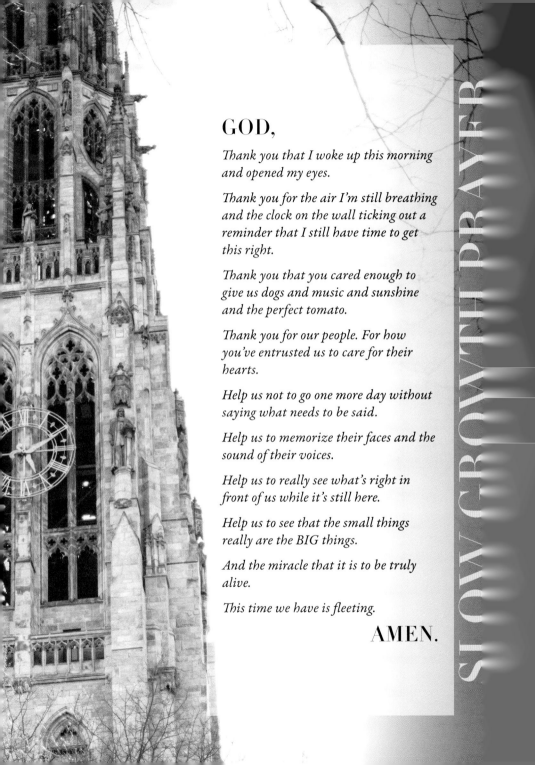

GOD,

Thank you that I woke up this morning and opened my eyes.

Thank you for the air I'm still breathing and the clock on the wall ticking out a reminder that I still have time to get this right.

Thank you that you cared enough to give us dogs and music and sunshine and the perfect tomato.

Thank you for our people. For how you've entrusted us to care for their hearts.

Help us not to go one more day without saying what needs to be said.

Help us to memorize their faces and the sound of their voices.

Help us to really see what's right in front of us while it's still here.

Help us to see that the small things really are the BIG things.

And the miracle that it is to be truly alive.

This time we have is fleeting.

AMEN.

SLOW GROWTH PRAYER

digging
DE

PART II

EP

letting go of not enough

you are chasing versions of you that you
thought you had to become

THESE ILLUSIONS
IN THE DISTANCE

What has a man
from all the toil
and striving of
heart with which
he toils beneath
the sun? For all his
days are full of sorrow,
and his work is a vexation.
Even in the night his heart
does not rest. This also is vanity.

ECCLESIASTES 2:22–23

THERE IS A PICTURE OF ME when I was nine, maybe ten years old.

My hair is long, but it is the kind of kinky-curly that could only be achieved through *permanent* chemical convincing. My shoes are dirty. My teeth are gapped. My big-hair bangs are in these short, disheveled ringlets resting way too high up on my forehead, as if someone pulled a fire alarm and they are trying desperately to run away panicked in every direction. They are fleeing their way toward the nearest emergency exits, which I assume must have been clearly marked on either side by my oversized ears.

THE
ILLUSIONIST

"This version of you is always up ahead of you, glowing in radiant gilded light from her mountaintop moments and lofty position on high."

I am, quite inexplicably, crouched down in a pose with both my elbows propped up on my knees and my chin resting on my fists, an angle that only serves to exaggerate the size of my father's nose planted squarely in the center of my face. If I can be certain of one thing to this day, it is that no one—*absolutely no one*—asked me to pose like that. My head looks way too big for my skinny little body. And when you add in the sheer size of the hair, it's amazing I could even hold my neck up. Which maybe explains the pose.

That was the beginning of the end for me.

Most people probably can't pinpoint the exact moment when their awkward phase began. Me? I have photographic evidence of the very minute I went from a cute kid to the *ugly* girl. It's an image that is burned into my brain. I can't unsee it.

I have carried that girl with me wherever I go.

There isn't a room I've walked into that I don't feel like she walks in first. There isn't a table I've tried to sit at where she hasn't already been laughed at and turned away. And every time I meet someone new, I feel like *she* is the girl they are seeing.

If I'm being really honest here, it took me years before I would even show that photo to anyone. It was like I was terrified that if they ever saw me like that, they too would never be able to unsee it. It would open their eyes to the ugly girl I really was standing before them, and they would never be able to see me as anything else. All the shame would come flooding back in.

And any illusion of the woman I was working so hard to become would be shattered in an instant.

YOU ARE CHASING VERSIONS of you that you thought you had to become. These illusions in the distance, a you that is not one. For every time you get closer, they splinter and divide. A diverging army of "supposed to be" whose only hope is that you hide.

But you were not called for chasing, this constant running, out of breath. You were called to stand on fertile ground made silent when they've left. These voices that are shouting, telling you everything you have to be. I hope one day you learn to love the voice that you call . . . "me."

There is this version of you off in the distance that you keep chasing.

She is better dressed, always showered, super organized, never running late, and her house and purse are always clean. Her skin is more glowy, she makes time to work out, she actually eats that neglected bag of kale sitting in the back of your refrigerator. There are no dark circles under her eyes, she always remembers to floss, and there is *never* a hair on her head out of place. She has color-coded goals written in her perfect swoop of handwriting. And she never misses a deadline. She's present, peaceful, intentional, has time for everything and everyone that matters. And everything she touches grows with limitless abundance until it is pure gold.

This version of you is always up ahead of you, glowing in radiant gilded light from her mountaintop moments and lofty position on high. You call out to her to wait for you—to let you catch up—as breathless and panicked you claw your way up the rocky ledge that divides you. Your knees are scraped and bruised now from the climb, your fingers raw and bloody. These broken nails are digging into your once wide-open palms, all in the name of this incessant clawing your way to the top, to some elusive high ground in the distance you have always called . . . *someday*. You fall down again and again, trying to reach her, until at last you find a rock to rest on and you determine to just *stay*.

She turns if only for a minute—white robes billowing in the pristine air surrounding her, her long hair floating but never seeming to

THE CONTORTIONIST

"Every day you are out there walking this tight-rope into a trapeze act, a contortionist twisting yourself up into tiny tethered knots, doing back-bends until your back breaks, trying to squeeze yourself into a corner that takes up even one inch less space in this world. Because to contort is easier than to be criticized."

THE

MASQUERADER

"You have become a master of disguise, masquerading in these qualifiers. Wearing all the different masks and all the different hats. Spinning plates and spinning fates and spinning out, but never once letting anything drop, including the act."

land—she stares you directly in the eyes, these dimly lit mirror reflections of her own. Smiles a sweet, superior smile. And then goes on without you.

You know that feeling of being left behind. Whether in a dream or a waking nightmare, you know the feeling of running after someone who would not stay. That pit pounding in your chest, the sputter of sobs rising up that steal your breath away, the familiar arms that once held you now always arm's length beyond your grasp. You know what it is to lose someone.

"Don't go. Don't go. Don't go."

But perhaps the greatest heartbreak of all is the day you lose yourself.

It's the day you realize there are a thousand supposed-to-be versions of you standing on a thousand illusioned, illuminated mountaintop moments in the distance. And not a single one of them cares enough about you to let you catch up. They go on without you, leave you where they found you—bloody, broken, and exhausted from the climb.

If I could hold a mirror up to you right now, this is what I would want you to see.

There are places in your life where you are shrinking into supposed-to-be, simply because it makes other people more comfortable. You want to be seen as smart, but not too smart. Serious, but not too serious. Silly, but not too silly. Loud, but not too loud. Quiet, but not too quiet. Ambitious, but not too ambitious. Successful, but not too successful.

Someone with opinions, but never too opinionated. Someone who is real, someone who is struggling, but never struggling too much.

Every day you are out there walking this tightrope into a trapeze act, a contortionist twisting yourself up into tiny tethered knots, doing backbends until your back breaks, trying to squeeze yourself into a corner that takes up even one inch less space in this world.

Because to contort is easier than to be criticized.

Too much. Too little. Too not enough. Too different from what they were expecting. These words ring in your ears like a silencing alarm, screaming out their every warning that there is something wrong with you right down to the wiring. And if you could just be less of something or more of something, it would be easier to go along and get along.

So you have become a master of disguise, masquerading in these qualifiers. Wearing all the different masks and all the different hats. Spinning plates and spinning fates and spinning out, but never once letting anything drop, including the act.

You find clever ways to hide right there in plain sight. But you are wilting. Withering in the glare of being held under the magnifying glass. And I get it.

It is because of the girl in the photo that I have spent way too long believing the lie that if I want to be accepted, I can never show up with even so much as a hair out of place.

Which has proven exceptionally difficult to execute for a girl with a lifelong history of such unruly hair.

GOD,

When I was writing these words, you revealed something that knocked me to my knees. It knocked the wind right out of me. How have I never seen it before?

This grown-up Girl After the Trailer version of me has been chasing a thousand supposed-to-be versions of herself in the distance, these superior beings living for the mountaintop moments, who only ever care enough to look down on her. And who never once slow down enough to let her catch up. She is not enough of something for them, God, so they go on without her. Leave her behind in the heartbreak of losing herself.

My eyes have been forever fixed on the horizon, always facing forward to the next high ground I can reach for. And yet I haven't once realized . . . all along this grown-up version of me has been doing the very same thing to that nine-going-on-ten little girl.

The Girl in the Trailer wasn't enough of something for me. All I could ever do was look down on her and try my best to leave her behind. Just as I have been reaching for a thousand supposed-to-be versions of us up ahead, all the while she has been reaching for me.

Help me to turn around, God. Help me to see. Help me to finally find myself . . . by not losing her.

AMEN.

SLOW GROWTH PRAYER

we believe these sophisticated powers of perception can see right through us

№

12

A HANNIBAL LECTER MONOLOGUE

> *"Who can hide in secret places so that I cannot see them?"* declares the LORD. *"Do not I fill heaven and earth?"*
>
> JEREMIAH 23:24

"CHEAP SHOES, CLARICE."

It probably wouldn't surprise you if I told you that *The Silence of the Lambs* is a movie that *haunted* me, stuck with me a long time after I first watched it.

But it wouldn't be for the reason you think.

Oh sure, it's a terrifying movie with plenty of jump-out-of-your-seat scenes. It's gory and suspenseful, nerve-racking in that psychological thriller sort of way. But as a lifelong scary movie fan going all the way back to "One, two, Freddy's coming for you," I eat that stuff for breakfast.

No, the real scene that stuck with me actually became famous to most of the world for an entirely different reason. Let's just say it involved some fava beans and a nice chianti. And again, that's horrifying and

113

gratuitous, not to mention wildly original, unexpected, and perfectly portrayed with cool callousness by one Sir Anthony Hopkins.

But what he says before that is the thing that really haunts me. In speaking to Jodie Foster's character, Agent Clarice Starling, he begins the monologue that would soon become known the world over.

> You're so ambitious, aren't you? But you know what you look like to me with your good bag and your cheap shoes? You look like a rube. A well-scrubbed, hustling rube with a little taste. Good nutrition has given you some length of bone, but you're not more than one genera- tion from poor white trash, are you, Agent Starling? And that accent you've tried so desperately to shed—pure West Virginia. What was your father, dear? Was he a coal miner? Did he stink of the lamp? And oh, how quickly the boys found you. All those tedious, sticky fum- blings in the back seats of cars, while you could only dream of getting out. Getting anywhere. Getting all the way to the FBI.*

When I talk about The Most Put-Together Woman in the Room, this is what I mean.

Remember, The Most Put-Together Woman in the Room doesn't walk in that way because she *feels* the most put-together. She walks in, aiming to have not a single hair out of place, because somehow, some- way, somewhere along the line she got it in her head that this was the *bare minimum standard* she had to hit just to *qualify* to walk into most rooms. Just to be eligible to have a seat at most tables.

And now every room she walks into, she feels like the people around her can see right through her, just like in this scene. Every place she goes, she feels like she is surrounded by a room full of well- meaning, well-adjusted, benign Hannibal Lecters with their matching pearls and highly sophisticated powers of perception. Feeling like at

* *The Silence of the Lambs*, directed by Jonathan Demme (Orion Pictures, 1991).

any minute one of them could turn on her, could look her up and down, and in one cool, casual monologue reduce her to a mere caricature of herself.

A well-scrubbed rube. One generation removed from what most of the world would dismiss as poor white trash. The hint of an accent. A good bag that only serves to draw attention by way of contrast to the cheap shoes. Further proof that she will always somehow come up just a little short in hiding who she once was. No matter how hard she tries, there will always be a dead giveaway.

She will always have a tell.

I spent years of my life fearing that for any room I walked into, anyone paying even the slightest bit of attention could instantly size me up as "poor white trailer trash." Whether it was something that I was wearing or the way I said something wrong or a social grace I had not yet learned. It was easy to fall down a rabbit hole in the shape of a dark, dingy well. My fingernails still broken and bleeding from the last time I tried to claw my way out.

I spent years of my life fearing that the world could see right through me.

And then I spent years more wondering why I ever cared.

I did grow up in a trailer. That's a part of who I am. And I have gone places since that trailer. That is also a part of who I am.

Why are we so quick to hide away the dark depths of our own story, believing it immediately disqualifies us? Why is it that we're only a fan of the underdog story when it comes to other people? Why is it that we can cheer for everyone else's overcoming story but our own?

The truth is, most of us are walking around with a Hannibal Lecter–worthy monologue on repeat in our own head. We hear that syrupy, serpentine voice hissing constant lies. It holds us under a microscope, perpetually scanning from head to toe looking for the proof

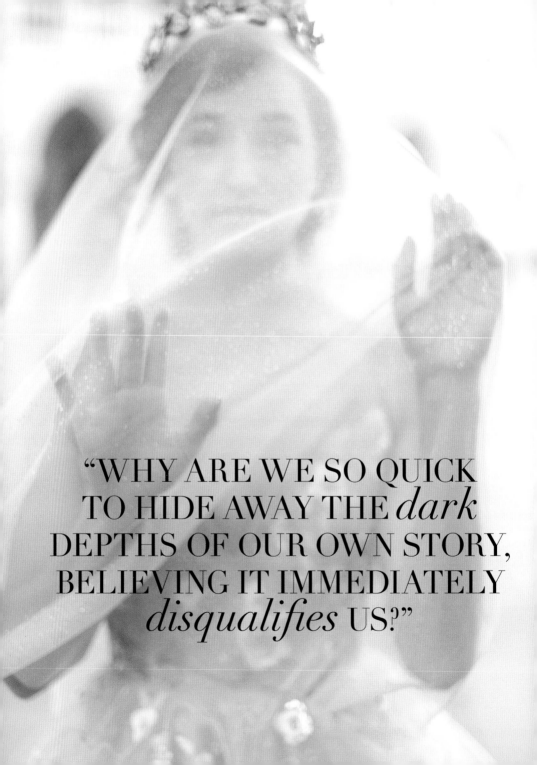

"WHY ARE WE SO QUICK TO HIDE AWAY THE *dark* DEPTHS OF OUR OWN STORY, BELIEVING IT IMMEDIATELY *disqualifies* US?"

that we haven't come as far as we thought we have, have we now? Getting out. Getting anywhere. Getting all the way to the very rooms we're standing in. That voice loves nothing more than to tell us we're right back where we started.

Even better if it makes us believe we never really left at all.

FOR MANY OF US, God sometimes feels like that cold, calculating observer behind the glass.

We sit there before him in our (Sunday) best suit and most sensible shoes, our hands clasped tightly together in our laps, praying that he doesn't see how bad they're shaking in the wake of his presence. We make our best attempt at small talk, knowing at any moment he could turn on us, could cast that devout stare in our direction. That those supernatural powers of perception he bears could easily slice and dice us up into tiny little pieces anytime he wants. He could look us up and down in a quick, divine once-over and immediately zero in on our deepest flaws, every fear and insecurity laid bare there before him, our deepest, most secret sins caught in the clutches of his gaze.

A lamb left waiting for the slaughter.

He feels dangerous up close, so we develop all these ways to keep him safe there at arm's length. These futile, transparent barriers between us. These security precautions we erect—as if they could ever contain him—all in the name of keeping his judgment from eating us alive.

A lot of us have gotten really good at psychoanalyzing God.

We've become experts in the field at assigning him all sorts of logic and laws that are not his own. We want to put God in a box. A shiny, six-by-eight cell of containment, a bulletproof barrier, one where he's over there and we're over here, and it works so long as all the people living in glass houses all around us promise to never throw stones.

This way we never truly have to come face-to-face with God, close enough to feel his breath on the hot flush and flesh of our cheeks. We can continue to escape his grasp if we will only play the role of thoughtful and discerning detective.

A purely intellectual relationship for a God who has always cared more about our heart.

The irony, of course, is that we're over here trying to hide, worried about a God who could cut us up into tiny little bite-size pieces if he only saw what we were really made of—every shame, every struggle, every doubt.

Meanwhile, Jesus, who saw everything, still came down and put on flesh—took on every hunger, every pain, the sting of death itself, this suffering in silence of the Lamb of God—just to be close to us.

And to once and for all tear down every one of these see-through walls that separate us.

GOD,

Thank you that although you could have chosen to see our every flaw, you instead sent your Son to be the perfect sacrifice so that we could be seen as spotless.

I can't imagine what it was like for Jesus. To have first experienced heaven, life free of all pain and hurt, free of every shame and betrayal and heartbreak. To be completely at one with you, God, no separation at all from your love.

For him to then intentionally and willingly put on flesh, to instantly feel how hard it can be to walk around this earth as fully human. To be tired. To be hungry. To be wounded and to bleed. To wonder if you had forsaken him.

Jesus took on and felt every last ounce of pain and suffering so that we could be free of it. Lord, forgive me for EVER believing you to be a distant God. An indifferent God. A God who loves to size me up and disqualify me from a safe distance behind the glass.

I don't want to hide in plain sight from you anymore, God. You already see every part of me and look on me with love.

My every pain and shame and fear at once goes quiet. This is the silence you offer; this is the sacrifice of the Lamb.

AMEN.

SLOW GROWTH PRAYER

№ 13

THEY LOVE ME,
THEY LOVE ME NOT

You have searched me,
LORD, and you know me.
You know when I sit and
when I rise; you perceive
my thoughts from afar. You
discern my going out and my
lying down; you are familiar with
all my ways. Before a word is on my
tongue you, LORD, know it completely.

PSALM 139:1–4

"WILL I EVER MATTER?"

You might be shocked if you knew how many times those words have spilled from my lips.

When the numbers are disappointing. When the answer I dreamed would be a yes is still a resounding no. When the shoulder is cold. When the door is slammed. When the engagement has tanked. When nobody really seems to care. When it feels like everyone else is hanging out without me.

121

All converging paths lead back to this one bless-ed, broken road I find myself walking without end: Will I ever be a person who *mattered* while she was here?

Sometimes I feel like I might disappear altogether.

There are days when I wish so badly to be *seen*. Seen by the people I look up to. Seen by the ones who are where I want to be. Seen by the ones who could tap me on the shoulder, tap me on the forehead, tap to tag me in that post, and suddenly I would be where they are. I would have finally *arrived*.

On those days when the approval doesn't come, when I disappear into the background noise of a thousand shouting voices, I feel like I may just disintegrate altogether. Dematerialize. A billion atomized molecules floating quietly into the roaring void. A vapor vanishing into the mist without warning.

The Bible tells us, "Yet you do not know what tomorrow will bring—what your life will be! For you are like a vapor that appears for a little while, then vanishes" (James 4:14 CSB).

Like I said: *this time we have is fleeting.*

So most of us are walking around with this urgent hope that our time here will matter. We all want our "one wild and precious life" to count for something.* We want to be seen. We want to be recognized. We hold this truth to be self-evident in our shaking hands: To be seen is to be known, and to be known is to be loved. A daisy chain of petals wilting and falling away, these threadbare strings unraveling faster than we can pull them.

And with raspy, bated breath we close our eyes and make a wish.

They love me, they love me not.

I feel like I've been waiting forty years for the world to answer yes to that question "Will I ever matter?" Forty years I've been wandering

*Mary Oliver, "The Summer Day," *Devotions* (New York: Penguin, 2017), 316.

in the wilderness of the world's approval. This dry, desolate, sand-scorched desert of withheld invitations and rescinded validations that leaves my throat parched and gasping for even the slightest drop of relief.

We already know the truth. It is dawning on us with each new day.

This moment of arrival is a mirage, an oasis of belonging always off in the distance, always just out of reach, always just beyond our fingertips. We will die first of this thirst for approval before the world will ever think to offer us a drink.

Let me be clear here. This desire to be deeply known and deeply loved is not wrong. It is wired into our very being. It is part of the original design and blueprint for how we were created.

It's just that we've been looking for it in all the wrong places.

We long to be known, we long to be loved, because it points back to that perfect relationship we can only find with God. We ache for something we can't find here. To paraphrase something C. S. Lewis said, the fact that our heart yearns for something earth can't supply is proof that heaven must be our home.

God at once knows everything about us—every hope, every dream, every fear, every flaw, every ugly, petty thought that flashes through our mind, the kind of thing that would make the world turn its back on us in an instant if it only knew. He sees all of it, and he loves us all the same. Unconditionally. Unequivocally. Without strings. Without fear. Never once holding back.

Psalm 139:1–4 says, "You have searched me, LORD, and you know me. You know when I sit and when I rise; you perceive my thoughts from afar. You discern my going out and my lying down; you are familiar with all my ways. Before a word is on my tongue you, LORD, know it completely."

You are familiar with all my ways. You perceive my thoughts from afar. Before a word is on my tongue you, Lord, know it completely.

When I read those words, when I really absorb what they mean, it makes my cheeks flush hot with embarrassment to think about God seeing every little thing like that. I instinctively drop my head, this involuntary reflex to the hammer of shame in pure knee-jerk reaction. It makes my eyes wince, closed up tight in an instant, at the very thought of the last ten thousand things that I've done wrong. Have you ever sat straight up in bed at three in the morning because your brain decided it was the perfect time to remind you of that one wrong thing you said to that one person that one time . . . five years ago? It's kind of like that. Times ten thousand.

And suddenly, disappearing—disintegrating altogether into the roaring void—doesn't seem like such a bad plan. Wandering in the desert wilderness alone starts to take on a certain new Thoreau-esque charm. This life of quiet desperation. We may never be seen, but hey . . . at least we won't be *exposed*. This becomes especially tempting for a girl who has gotten really good at hiding in plain sight.

But God was prepared for that.

"'Who can hide in secret places so that I cannot see them?' declares the Lord. 'Do not I fill heaven and earth?'" (Jer. 23:24).

Besides, if we try to hide, we miss the best part. To be seen is to be known . . . *and to be known is to be loved.*

It makes my breath catch in my throat to think about how, despite it all, I am still loved like that by God. Here is this laundry list of indictments I am more than guilty of every single day. I have spent so much of this life chasing things that do not ultimately matter. Trying to find worth in this fleeting currency that does not last. Wishing that other people's good things were my own.

We have been wandering in a desert of our own making, searching for approval in all the wrong places.

And it still doesn't change a single thing.

God sees it all. Knows every part. And loves us just the same.

GOD,

Thank you that every time the world looks right through us, casts their gaze beyond us as if we aren't even there, you see us.

You know us.

And in an instant, we are loved.

Thank you for all the ways you lead us out of these deserts of our own making, these wastelands of wasted time that is already so fleeting.

We wander aimlessly, seeking approval and validation.

We are at once terrified that people can see right through us, while being even more afraid of never being truly seen.

I'm so tired of pulling at these loose threads, Lord.

They love me, they love me not.

We were never meant to live this way.

You know every little thing about me, and still you say I am worthy.

Help me to live my life from this place, God.

Help me to live seen, known, and loved.

Because it turns out love is the antidote to shame.

AMEN.

№

14

IT TURNS OUT WE'RE
ALL PRETTY THIRSTY

*you have the God of the universe in your corner—
it's time to stop chasing people*

Am I now trying to win the approval of human beings, or of God?

I SAW A QUOTE on Pinterest once that read something to the effect of, "You have worked too hard and come too far for people to still be unsure about you."

I felt that.

On a deep, metaphysical, cellular level. It was like every mitochondrion in my body was vibrating in unison. They were reverberating with an atomic-level slow clap, as if they were sitting in the middle of a cafeteria scene of some high school musical. I half expected one of them to jump up on the table and proclaim its love for the prom queen. Or, you know, start a fistfight with a lunch tray Cobra Kai style, as the case may be. My head began nodding. I quickly took a screenshot and sent it to my producer, Elizabeth.

We had *just* been talking about this.

Here I feel like I need to pause. This is one of those moments, like a Sharpie-mark-through-the-calendar line in the sand. Inevitably, two groups are going to emerge here. There are going to be the people who read a quote like that, tilt their head to the side, brow ever so subtly furrowed in confusion, nodding but only slightly, feeling like they don't quite get it yet.

And then there are going to be those of us who will have to be physically restrained from jumping on a lunchroom table ourselves. Or, at the very least, from pulling a Judd Nelson at the end of *The Breakfast Club* fist pump at the #truth we've just read.

We are the group who have spent our whole lives being just a little bit underestimated. Counted out. Baby in her pink dress, stuck somewhere in a dark corner at Kellerman's while the rest of the world dances center stage.

We are the kind ones. The quiet ones. The perpetual hard workers. The ones who took a little bit longer to get here. And we are tired, right down to our bones, of other people not seeing the pure 24-karat gold potential we hold inside us from having already walked through the fire.

We know what we are capable of. And we know where we are headed. But at the same time, we're weary from the chase, this running after other people and hoping we will someday be enough of something to be invited to sit with them.

I had a dream the other night where I was running after an author I look up to. For what felt like hours upon hours, I tried to push my way through the crowd to catch up to her, to get close enough to her that I could place my first book, *Dirt*, gently in her waiting hands. I would thumb through the chapters until I found the perfect passage, this ticket to belonging in proper paragraph form.

But every time I got close enough, she was always just out of reach.

And with bated breath
we close our eyes and make a

WISH.

They love me, they love me not.

All I wanted was for her to turn around and turn the page. To really *see* me. To open up these words and find my heart poured out there in tiny letters and wraparound paragraphs, tucked between the one-inch guardrails of the set standard margins. This work that was no less than a lifetime in the making. In my dream scenario she would look me in the eye, tell me that I have what it takes. She would see something in me worth calling out and she would speak life to it. And just like that, I could stop running.

Instead, I woke up exhausted.

For so many of us, we feel like we have come too far and worked too hard for people to still be unsure of us. We crave approval and belonging. To be seen and really known. We want just one person we admire to be able to see everything we've done, to see how far we've come, to see something in us that is good and call it worthy.

Oh, but don't miss this.

In doing that, we are equating "something in us that is good" with something we have *done*. We are acting as if our very worth is inherently tied to what we do. Something we have created, something we have accomplished, a certain level of excellence we have achieved. A box that we have finally checked.

Did I believe that author in my dream should turn around and see me simply because I am a fellow human being worthy of the same love, dignity, and respect that she is? No. I believed she should turn around and see me because I had finally done something that made me worthy of being seen. I believed that if she would actually read these words I wrote, see for herself that they are good . . . then *I* would somehow suddenly be good enough too.

What does that say I believe about myself? And what does it say I believe about every other person around me too?

This crowd I was chasing her through, pushing my way past to get her attention—did I ever really *see* any of them? Did I stop to turn around, look even one of them in the eye, and call out something good I saw in *them*? No, they were just an obstacle getting in my way. Standing between me and the approval I was so desperately chasing after. I was too busy trying to be seen . . . to ever really see anyone else.

All the while we're out there chasing people, we forget there may be people right now who are chasing us. We forget to turn around.

Meanwhile, God has never once asked us to chase after him. He has never been unsure of us or of the purpose and plan he has for our lives. We have never once had to fight to belong with him or push our way past anyone else to reach him. The table has already been set before us and there is more than enough room for everybody. With him we are known and we are loved down to every slow-clapping cell in our body. He created us from the very beginning of our being, looked at his creation and called it good.

Once again I am reminded: to be seen is to be known, and to be known is to be loved.

A lot of us have been waiting for the world to take notice of our work. But what if we flipped that equation on its head?

What if we instead asked ourselves, "What is the work we would create even if *no one* was looking?"

If it was only about using the work of our hands as an offering to God—to thank him for always seeing and knowing and loving us so well—what would we build then? If we took every gift he gave us and gave it right back to him, how would that change our words and our

99

I WAS TOO BUSY TRYING TO BE SEEN . . . TO EVER REALLY SEE ANYONE ELSE.

songs, our pictures and our paintings? Would every brushstroke become a whisper of worship? Every paragraph a psalm of poetry and praise etched from the deep valleys of our pain?

I want to stop crawling through the desert. I want to stop chasing elusive grains of sand and instead remind myself that this time is slipping away. I want to stop begging the world for barely a drop of water and turn my face to the well where I will never be thirsty again.

We're waiting for the world to finally tell us that we matter. But the thing is, *most* people are so busy walking around wanting to be seen and loved themselves that they forget to ever really see anyone else.

It turns out, we're all pretty *thirsty*.

We're all just walking that dusty broken road home. Waiting for that moment of arrival. Waiting for the answer to be yes.

"Will I ever matter?"

Stop for a minute, turn around, and ask God how he sees it. He'll tell you.

You already do.

You have the God of the universe in your corner, believing in you and what you are capable of in him.

What on earth are you doing still chasing people?

GOD,

I want to thank you for all the ways we never have to chase you.

You never play games with us. You never withhold your love or approval, hoping to put us in our place. Hoping to keep us small.

You see how far we've come, Lord. And you see how hard we're working. And— help us to not miss this—neither of those changes a thing about how much you have always loved us.

When we want to place these dreams of ours in your waiting hands, you are not always somewhere up ahead, always just out of reach.

You are right there waiting with open arms.

You have never been unsure of us. You've never asked us to pay a few more dues before we are enough of something to sit with you.

You lean down close and can't wait to hear all about it.

You see every good thing in us and you speak it out.

Yours is the voice whispering in our hearts on repeat: "You already matter. It's already enough."

AMEN.

SLOW GROWTH PRAYER

15

"i'm not ——— enough" turns into
"sure, but it's easy for her"

MAKE ME A BIRD,
SO I CAN FLY AWAY

*Consider how the wild flowers grow.
They do not labor or spin. Yet I tell
you, not even Solomon in all his
splendor was dressed like one of these.*

LUKE 12:27

THERE IS A FLOCK of small, black birds outside
my window right now.

They are in the thin strip of grass across from our
house, which in turn faces out to the Long Island
Sound. One of the things I love most about living here
is that every day the water can be wildly different from
the day before. Some days it is a pastel blue, the color
of Cézanne or Degas. On those days, it is so glassy
smooth it looks like a painted-on scene instead of
something alive and real. Until you get close enough to
see the small brushstrokes of undercurrents that make
up the whole, and then you realize the water will never
be content to be defined by the world as just one thing.

Other days the water is violent, churning out a
thrashing, murky green torrent of waves that give way

to long flowing whitecaps—the wispy, whipping locks of the old man and the sea.

Then there are the days when it is like a water ballet in motion, graceful arms reaching out from the depths, these John Singer Sargent hands stretching ever upward toward heaven in a posture of prayer and praise.

Today the water is a steely gray. Thick and slow-moving like dense fog. It looks like you could reach out and slice right through it, where I can only imagine it would sit up on its own in your spoon, shivering yet somehow still solid like sweet crème brûlée. The steel of the water gives way to a slightly lighter gray sky above, an exercise in monochrome divided only by a key line of dark navy vanishing point by point at the horizon.

The birds are moving in a pack. Alternating fits of flight or frenzy, landing on the soggy wet ground to feed for only a moment before taking off again. They are an elegant symphony of movement orchestrated in perfect measure. I continue to be amazed that they never mistime the landing and crash right into one another. There is not a doubt in my mind, if I were a bird that's exactly how it would go.

I look at those birds, so unhurried and unworried in the promise that each day they will be provided for. And never have I ever wanted to be a bird more. But not only for the freedom of flight. For the freedom of knowing—finally believing with my whole heart—that there is enough for all of us. More than enough to go around.

Jesus tells us, "Look at the birds of the air; they do not sow or reap or store away in barns, and yet your heavenly Father feeds them. Are you not much more valuable than they? Can any one of you by worrying add a single hour to your life?" (Matt. 6:26–27 NIV).

I'm here to tell you that if it *were* possible to add a single hour to your life by worrying, I would live to be approximately 1,976 years old.

So much of this trying to achieve our way into worth is born out of a scarcity mentality. It's a zero-sum, someone-else-is-going-to-get-my-

"LOOK AT THE *birds*
OF THE AIR....
ARE YOU NOT MUCH MORE
valuable THAN THEY?"

—Matthew 6:26–27

piece-of-the-pie way of seeing the world. It's this lie we hold on to that *her* success is going to directly and adversely impact mine. She is already doing that thing I want to do. She is already doing it better and is better known for it. Why would the world ever need me and what I have to say when her voice is already so loud in the room?

Out of that scarcity-scorched earth, a new lie begins to take root: *Sure, but it's easy for her.*

Sure, but she's younger.

Sure, but she was able to go full time with her business.

Sure, but she's married and her spouse's income covers all the bills.

Sure, but she's pretty.

Sure, but she's established.

Sure, but she's outgoing and an extrovert.

Sure, but she doesn't have kids, so she has more time.

Everything we think makes *her* story easier is really a commentary about what we believe to be lacking in *ours*.

"Sure, but it's easy for her" mixes with the murky waters of "But I'm not _____ enough."

We worry that we're too late. We worry that we're too behind. We worry that we've messed up too much. Made too many mistakes. Come up short too many times. We've fallen down seven times, and we're not sure we can bring ourselves to get back up for round eight.

We have tried with everything in us to achieve our way into worth, and when we finally reach the end of ourselves we look out the window and we remember the birds. How they did not sow or reap or store away or do anything else to deserve God having a plan for their lives, a plan to provide everything they need.

And yet there they are, a symphony in flight. Wings unencumbered by the weight of every little thing they didn't do. These simple creatures who still somehow know freedom.

And never have I ever wanted to be a bird more.

GOD,

Set me free of not believing. Set me free of this doubt that is always churning there right below the surface, this part of me that cannot grasp and hold on to the hope that you have a plan for my life.

Help me to believe that this plan of yours is right on time. Help me to trust that it has been perfectly orchestrated.

Let me set my life as a worship song to you, Lord. Every movement a posture of prayer and praise to your holy name.

Help me to hope good things for others more than I think about myself.

In you, there truly is more than enough to go around.

Help me to stop crashing into other people. To remember that "she" is not my enemy. We are all parts of the same body, moving together in a pack.

This symphony in motion.

Wings unencumbered by our doubts.

Help me to know freedom like that, Lord.

Set me free of me.

AMEN.

SLOW GROWTH PRAYER

№ 16

eventually, my antidote to scarcity becomes an exercise in excess

THAT VERSION
OF ME IS INSATIABLE

*Their end is destruction,
their god is their belly, and
they glory in their shame, with
minds set on earthly things.*

PHILIPPIANS 3:19

Insatiable (adj.): incapable of being satisfied;
synonyms: unappeasable; unquenchable.*

SOMETIMES I FEEL like I'm suffering from spiritual amnesia.

I can have these powerful moments of clarity where God shows me exactly the life he wants for me. *The use of my gifts . . . in service to others . . . for the rest of my life . . . for his ultimate glory.* That's it.

It's a message that God has been showing me over and over on repeat for most of my adult life, apparently because I keep forgetting. Eugene Peterson called this life "a long obedience in the same direction," and Oswald Chambers said it was "my utmost for his

Merriam-Webster, s.v. "insatiable," accessed May 19, 2021, https://www
.merriam-webster.com/dictionary/insatiable.

highest."* But it was Grandma Goldie, perhaps, who put it the most directly of all: "Mary Ellen, how you do anything is how you do everything."

In these moments it all becomes so clear to me—like a warm, golden, engulfing light. And my shoulders relax, retreating at once from the rocky shore of my jawline. My forehead softens. My heart stops racing. That voice in my head telling me that no matter what I do it will never be enough at once goes quiet.

In these moments I know what I'm here for. I know what I have been created for. There is no hurry. There is no rush. I am not in a race. There is no timeline of what society says I have yet to accomplish in order to matter in someone else's eyes. There is only this day in front of me. And the work of my hands I have been called to do.

But then just as quickly as it all becomes clear . . . I forget.

I forget what God says success looks like, and I take up the world's definition again instead. This frantic, frenzied pace. This roar shouting into the void, like someone standing upon a house of sand and screaming at the ocean to hold back the waves. Or a woman who is dying of thirst and keeps trying to get her fill by drinking directly from the fire hose. Suddenly all I care about is wanting everything I don't already have.

I once told my goals coach, Kim, that it's like there are two versions of me, one stacked inside the other like those Russian nesting dolls. At my core is the person who wants to spend her days in unhurried work, pursuing excellence in honor of God. She's at peace. She lives a life of obedience. She knows that the things of this world won't be the things that last.

The only problem is, that person is tucked inside this whole other version of me. The one who wants to achieve and perform, compare

*Eugene Peterson, *A Long Obedience in the Same Direction* (Downers Grove, IL: InterVarsity, 1983); Oswald Chambers, *My Utmost for His Highest* (1927), www.utmost.org.

HONOR THE
FOUNDATION ON
WHICH WE STAND

N°3

the antidote to more is noticing
all we already have

THIS WORK OF GIVING UP ACHIEVING FOR OUR WORTH,

it doesn't happen all at once.

worth

LIKE ANYTHING WE HAVE BECOME ADDICTED TO,

it is a choice we have to make over and over . . .

ONE DAY AT A TIME.

and compete my way into mattering. And that outer version of me is the one who has access to the world.

That version of me is *insatiable*. Unquenchable. Thirsty. And incapable of believing there is *any* amount of more that will ever be enough.

This is the version of me that wants to stuff my life so full—absolutely filled to the brim with commitments and calendars and clothes and things—that I never have to feel empty again. It's like I can't get enough. Dopamine is my drug of choice, and I am running on a forever high of doing it all. I'm flying down the road ninety miles an hour with my hair on fire.

And I like the way it burns.

Every day I'm out there walking around like a bundle of raw, exposed nerve endings. Every firing synapse is an exercise in scarcity, telling me that I'm running out of time to check enough boxes to ever really matter. Whispering how I'm late to a game with a score that was already stacked against me.

Until eventually, my only antidote to scarcity becomes this experiment in excess.

My overstuffed closets rain down on me in stacks of clothes there could never be enough versions of me to wear. My calendar is a whole sash full of merit badges, this busy turned badge of honor, where I have *always* won the prize for being the top cookie seller. Peddling in these sugary-sweet highs of getting everything I ever wanted. And getting everyone else around me as addicted as I am.

A few months ago, we were in the middle of launching something new. The *newest* new thing in a long line of crossing items off the list and getting things done. And I was tired. Bone-dry and exhausted. Scraping the bottom of a barrel that had already been lit on fire and burned through from the inside out. Until all I was left with were these little charred pieces of rusty metal turned ash to throw as my confetti. This ashes-to-ashes version of myself floating away on the breeze.

Right then my phone buzzed with a message from my good friend Nicole.

> Mary, I am so proud of you! You never cease to amaze me. But what I need you to hear right now is this . . . I *love* you way more than I am impressed by you (and that's saying a lot!).

I instantly burst into tears.

They rolled down my cheeks and puddled at my earlobes.

And just like that, somehow these small pools of saltwater were enough—at least for a little while—to extinguish every raw, exposed nerve ending. Every synapse on fire, burning itself up for the whole world's approval. They were silenced, if only for an instant, by this cool salve-to-the-wound of being seen, known, and loved by one real friend.

This work of giving up achieving for our worth, it doesn't happen all at once. Like anything we have become addicted to, it is a choice we have to make over and over . . . one day at a time. And in the process it can be so easy to forget who we really are.

My advice?

Surround yourself with people who see the magic in you and will remind you every chance they get.

In a world full of microscopes, your people should be mirrors. Mirrors show you who you are and who you are becoming. Microscopes hold you in one place for easier scrutiny.

Learn that difference early and remind yourself often.

And then be thankful for the mirrors in your life.

GOD,

Thank you for how you are the ultimate mirror in our lives, one where we can always see things clearly.

But I also want to take a minute today and thank you for the human mirrors that you, in your incredible kindness, have placed in our lives.

Those true friends who are with us and for us in every season of life.

The ones who love us way more than they are impressed with us. The ones who care more about us and who we are becoming than anything we can do for them.

God, this world can sometimes feel like we are pinned down, perpetually under the microscope. Insects caught in the glaring heat of the magnifying glass.

Thank you for the ones whose words are like cool salve in the face of the burn.

Thank you for the gift of friendship, God.

It is but a glimpse of the friend we have in you.

AMEN.

N<u>o</u>

17

INSECURITY REARS HER LOVELY HEAD

suddenly it feels safer to create nothing than to create failure

*For the righteous falls
seven times and rises again,
but the wicked stumble
in times of calamity.*

PROVERBS 24:16

MOST OF US ARE SO AFRAID of failing that we never even start.

There, I said it.

Now we can deal with it.

The irony for overachievers, of course—who normally feel pretty miserable and worthless unless we're out there, you know, *achieving*—is that when faced with the prospect of failure, it suddenly feels safer for us to do nothing than to risk coming up short. We feel paralyzed. We feel stuck. We become experts in avoidance. We would rather not even try, not even go after something, not even break ground on building the dream, than have to deal with the pain of things not working out.

It suddenly feels safer to create nothing than to create failure.

The world is absolutely stuffed full with self-preserving achievers. We're out there slow-limping around, pretending like we don't have a dream, our eyes glazed over with the look of someone who has forgotten what it feels like to really be alive, bumping up against our excuses over and over on repeat like some sort of walking dead. We are sleepwalking our way through our own lives, all in the name of saving face.

Recently I was with a friend, and we got to talking about all the ways we get in our own heads when it comes to getting started on a dream.

We think it's already been done. We think it's already been done better. We think it's already been done by someone the world actually wants to pay attention to. We think to ourselves, "Who is *ever* going to care about this?"

Insecurity rears her lovely head.

She flips her perfect hair, looks out from the four corners of her squares of influence, and smiles a Crest-whitestrip smile in our direction. All the while whispering about how we'll never be enough of something in order to have something to say. Not skinny enough, not young enough, not pretty enough, not outgoing enough.

So we take all those gifts that have been burning up inside us and hide them away again, a light under a basket. We go back to sleeping on a dream that has already been a lifetime in the making. But we're forgetting the most important part.

People who want to serve . . . *start.*

Now, here is where I am supposed to tell you to put your identity in Christ and everything will be fine. That if you just ring that bell, check that box, you'll finally be able to stop worrying about all these insecurities and find freedom like you never knew. And it's not even that this statement isn't true. *It is. It very much is.*

People who want to serve . . . start.

serve

start

It's just that for years I had no idea what that phrase "identity in Christ" was even supposed to mean. I mean, what are we actually talking about here? For a long time, whenever I heard somebody say it—which was often and on repeat and always in fluent Christian-speak—all I could bring myself to picture was some sort of heavenly driver's license. This proper photo identification given to you from the front of the line at a DMV located somewhere just south of the promised land. A laminated permit. A pretty, placarded permission slip summing up all the most important information about you and guaranteeing to the rest of the believing world that you aren't a fraud. This fake (it through the hard stuff) ID that you might have to whip out at a moment's notice, anytime someone felt like carding you to make sure you still belong.

"It's okay, my identity is in Christ! You can still serve me here."

In case it isn't clear, this card-carrying Christian version of identity misses the whole point.

Finding my identity in Christ was never about hitting every goal or never coming up short. It was never about the circles of people where I would suddenly belong or the tables that had always been all booked up before now suddenly having a seat for me. It's about knowing in the depths of my bones that I belong with God *no matter what else happens.*

> *THE GOD WHO IS IN YOU AND WITH YOU AND FOR YOU HAS ALREADY WON THE BATTLE OVER FEAR, DRIVEN IT OUT WITH PURE, PERFECT, UNCONDITIONAL LOVE.*

And it changes everything.

When you realize that God made you the way you are—every strength, every weakness, every single character in your story written on purpose *for* a purpose, every last hair on your head already accounted for—when you realize that, all those other circles fall away.

They can see you or they can *not* see you.

They can clap for you or they can *not* clap for you.

They can invite you in or they can keep on slamming the door.

They can look at you and see something worthy, something worth speaking life into, or they can go right on underestimating everything you bring to the table.

Either way.

Who you are, what you have been called to, the gifts you have been given, the places you are being asked to go—they are a foregone conclusion to God. Absolutely independent of the approval, sanction, check marks, influence, or invitations of anyone else. He made you, he sees you, and he for one feels *delight* when he looks at you. And once you realize that, there will be no more failing. Because failing is really just the fear of what other people will say if it doesn't work out the first time. It's not so much the falling on our faces that we're afraid of; it's the fear of falling on our faces in front of everyone else.

But when we operate from this place of who God says we are and where he says we are going, we can move forward with freedom. We can move forward free of fear over what the outcome may be.

We can try, we can stumble, we can fall down, we can rise again. We are *free* to have it take as long as it takes. Fall down seven times, get back up eight. But what we can't do is stay here. What we can't do is let this fear keep us standing still.

Right now you may be so caught up in all your fears, doubts, and insecurities—in all the ways it could go wrong and who might have something to say about it—that you are *missing* who it could help.

Head up. Eyes on what matters. You are *bigger* than the worst of your doubts. And this work you are being asked to do is far more important than the worst of your critics. Because the God who is in you and with you and for you has already won the battle over fear, driven it out with pure, perfect, unconditional love. There are no strings attached to trip you up. There are no hoops forcing you to jump forever higher. There is just a path carved out for you and you alone. And God is asking only that you take the first step.

You're so focused on what it is you're missing, what you're not "enough" of, that you can't even *start*. What if today you instead thought about all the people it would *serve*? Believe in that, hold on to that, and begin.

Because people who want to serve . . . *start*. ▓

GOD,

Thank you for the mud that is in our stories and the dirt paths you carve out for each and every one of us.

I thank you that before any of us ever breathed our first breath, there was a purpose you stitched into our lungs.

You wrote it on our hearts.

You carved it in the stars.

Thank you for walking that dirt path beside us, even as it leaves marks all up and down your crisp, white robes.

Thank you for being a God who is in the gritty. A God who walks alongside us even when the road seems long and the destination uncertain, even when we continue to trip over our own excuses again and again.

You are the God who reaches out a hand when we stumble. Who lifts us up and offers us rest when we need it. And then points us on our way again to the wide-open spaces you are calling us to.

There is no fear in you, God, and so long as we are following where you lead us, there is no failure either.

Only another chance to hold on to your hand, dust ourselves off . . . and rise again.

AMEN.

SLOW GROWTH PRAYER

now we are only as good or bad as the latest good thing that has happened to us

№ 18

18

THE GIRL WHO ALWAYS COMES THROUGH

I am the vine; you are the branches. If you remain in me and I in you, you will bear much fruit; apart from me you can do nothing. If you do not remain in me, you are like a branch that is thrown away and withers.

JOHN 15:5-6 NIV

THERE IS A FLIP SIDE to the girl who never gets started.

At some point, we become the girl who always comes through.

We have worked hard enough, excelled long enough, added enough A-pluses to our permanent record, that somewhere along the line the expectation among everyone around us has now become, "You've got this! You'll do it. Of course you will. You'll pull out another win just in time like you always do. That's just who you are."

This is meant as an encouragement, of course, a "look how much belief I hold in you" pep talk. A "let me tell you what I think you need to hear to keep going" anthem.

I only wish people knew what it felt like.

These words soak into my ears and burn down the back of my throat as I swallow yet another dose of the expectations this world has learned to put on me. A lesson, I am fully aware, that they have been taught by the disciplined instruction of my own hands. I have people-pleased and deadline-squeezed and overachieved my way into not really being human in their eyes anymore. I am a machine. An overproducing, overcommitted, overworked assembly line cranking out an ever endless supply of more. So why should I be surprised that *more* is what they now expect of me?

When I hear "You've got this!" all I can think is, "What if I don't, though? What if this is the time when I don't come through? What if I do come up short? What if I do disappoint you?"

And then come the inevitable questions hiding in plain sight right behind all the others.

"If that happens . . . would it be okay? Would you still love me anyway? Am I someone worth loving *apart* from what I can do for you? Am I someone worth loving apart from what I can deliver, accomplish . . . *achieve*?"

It used to be that our days were defined as good or bad by the latest good thing that happened to us.

But somewhere along the way, we started to believe that *we* are now only as good or bad as the latest good thing we have achieved.

I have known what it is to be so bone-tired that all you can do is curl up in a ball and press your face to the cold hardwood floor. Your shallow breath keeping time with the clock on the wall, this perpetual metronome machine ticking out all the time in the world that you lie there wasting away. You are but a candle with all the wax poured out, burning yourself down to the very end of your own rope, all in the name of casting some semblance of light into this dark, uncertain world. You lie there nearly spent as the last flickers dance against a pale blue wall, and you wonder, "Why is it okay for everyone else to burn out but me?"

> ❝ WE HAVE OFFICIALLY BECOME MORE AFRAID OF WHO WE ARE IF WE DISAPPOINT SOMEONE THAN WHAT HAPPENS WHEN WE BURN OUT.

But there is no time. You don't stay there and wait for an answer to come. You get back up and you get to work.

Because *that's just who you are.*

For a lot of us, A-plus has become our new standard baseline. The low-water mark that everyone around us has come to count on. The bare minimum standard they always expect to see. This, of course, packs a double whammy. It means that (a) we live daily with the crushing weight of impossibly high expectations (mostly our own), but (b) we are rarely celebrated, appreciated, or praised when we do reach them. *Of course you turned in a 100 percent performance. You always do.*

The grades have all been counted, the class curve is in, and it turns out that—at least for us—perfection is now the new *average.*

So we spin out, spilling every last drop of our blood, sweat, and tears in the name of keeping the streak alive. Now that we have impressed someone, we never *ever* want to be the one to let them down. We have officially become more afraid of who we are if we disappoint someone than what happens when the flame finally burns out.

For me this really boils down to two lies I have had playing in my head on repeat for as long as I can remember: (1) Everybody is counting on me to be perfect. (2) I can't count on anybody but myself.

Somewhere from the four corners of my mind, I hear Grandma Goldie's voice come back to whisper, "I'll do it myself." And in that moment, her exercise in stubbornness rings more like a love song to self-sufficiency. This is who we are now. This is what it means to be a strong woman. Straighten your spine, put an iron rod where all the vertebrae used to be, and let's get back to this backbreaking work of proving to the world that we don't need them.

When I talk to God about this, he reminds me of the branches.

"I am the vine; you are the branches. If you remain in me and I in you, you will bear much fruit; apart from me you can do nothing. If you do not remain in me, you are like a branch that is thrown away and withers" (John 15:5–6 NIV).

Of course, I've found myself yet again facedown on the floor. Of course, I've found myself yet again withering under the weight of the world's expectations. I have once again convinced myself that it is better to go it alone than to count on anybody, and that includes God.

I'm going to be honest with you: for a long time I considered that vine a shackle. As someone who is *good* at getting things done, it felt insulting to me that I had to be tied down this way. "Why can't you be a safety net instead of a tether, God? Be there to catch me if I fall. But otherwise, why can't you just let me fly?"

It took a long time for me to realize—and really it's something I'm still working on—that this vine was never about living in chains. We need God the same way we need food, sleep, and water . . . go too long without any of them and we start to fade away. Designing us to be dependent on him was God's way of reminding us that we never have to go it alone. There is always someone we can count on besides ourselves. We can count on him. He's going to show up. He's going to be faithful. He's going to be the "always more" when we have nothing left to give. More than that, he's going to point us to the fruit, reminding us of the good things we're growing.

And most important of all, he's going to tell us when it's *enough*.

Regardless of what the world might expect.

GOD,

I just want to take a minute to thank you. Because when I picture that vine now, all I can see is pure power rising up.

This hope springs eternal growing out of dry earth.

I tether myself to you, and once again I can feel a life force coursing through my veins.

This vine that has held me is no shackle.

This vine is color and freedom and fire and dirt.

When I plug into you, it's like I am plugging into the ultimate energy source. Not a power grid based on my output and scarcity, but an unending abundant supply that is not dependent on my performance.

You bring life, Jesus. You meet me in the scorched earth of heavy expectations and instead decide to do a new thing in the wilderness.

I abide in you.

I stay connected to you.

And every other good thing I am growing flows directly from that.

AMEN.

SLOW GROWTH PRAYER

these two-dimensional paper dolls start
to form the perfect woman in my mind

№ 19

MY JUDGE WEARS
A DRAPER JAMES
DRESS

Remember the Sabbath day, to keep it holy. Six days you shall labor, and do all your work, but the seventh day is a Sabbath to the LORD your God.

EXODUS 20:8–10

MY JUDGE WEARS a Draper James dress.

You would think that, having gone to law school and studied actual legal cases with precedent and Supreme Court decisions, it would be safe to assume that the imaginary judge who resides and presides in my head would wear long, black, flowing robes. Possibly a powdered wig. Maybe even a dissent collar.

But the truth is, my judge is much more concerned with a whole other kind of majority opinion.

My judge is an amalgamation. She is a paper doll, cut out from the pages of what is working for everyone else. She is a walking, talking dream board compiled from a collage of other people's beautiful lives. She is a whole that is somehow greater than the sum of her parts—this bright and airy home taken from a page ripped right out of the Pottery Barn catalog, a spread from the *Southern Living* vacation guide complete with crystal blue waters, a "how to wear it" insert from the Reese's Favorite Things collection. And then in some sort of mix of alchemy meets *Weird Science*, these two-dimensional ideal cutouts start to form the perfect woman in my mind.

A woman I could never *possibly* live up to.

That woman is my judge.

My judge has *opinions*, most of which revolve around how I'm not doing nearly enough. There is always someone doing more. There is always someone doing better. And she can't for the life of her understand why I just can't get it together like they have.

In the face of this inner critic, my self-preservation mode kicks into overdrive. Every time it tells me I'm not enough of something, I determine to just work harder. For a while there, I actually convince myself that the answer can be found at the end of a longer to-do list. It can be found at the end of a longer workday. It can be found in a life filled with far more hustle and much less heart. I convince myself I can actually outpace the speed at which my judge hands out her sentences.

And for a while there, it works.

But inevitably all these longer to-do lists and longer workdays leave me back on the familiar ground of barely hanging on at the end of my

> *MY JUDGE IS AN AMALGAMATION. SHE IS A PAPER DOLL, CUT OUT FROM THE PAGES OF WHAT IS WORKING FOR EVERYONE ELSE.*

rope. I have exhausted myself in these appeals. I plead for mercy. All my defenses need rest.

And now my judge really holds me in contempt.

Because of all the crimes I could commit, in her eyes rest is the worst offense of all.

ACHIEVING IS LIKE our oxygen.

Perfectionism is the penance we pay for taking up space in any room.

We don't choose to achieve, and we don't do it to feel better than anyone else. We do it because somewhere, somehow, a switch got flipped in us. Something broke inside. On a very profound level. And we're not going back. Shattered into a million pieces. Like a mirror when we weren't ready to deal with the reflection. And every day we're out there checking things off a list, that's just us trying to put ourselves back together again. Shard by jagged shard.[*]

I wrote these words in *Dirt* because it was important to me that people truly understand how visceral, primal, *survival* achieving can become for those of us who are running from a muddy part of our story. I think so often it can be easy for the world to look at these stories of people who didn't grow up with a lot or in the best of circumstances, people who then went on to accomplish big things, and just assume the only side effect is success.

It isn't.

The side effect, the whole dang disease really, is not knowing how to stop.

There is some deep, damaged place inside our brain—here I like to imagine the neural synapses firing like a downed power line in the

[*]Marantz, *Dirt*, 223.

middle of a thunderstorm, throwing a cascade of sparks in every direction and threatening to burn anyone who dares get too close. So that for those of us who feel hardwired to achieve and achieve and achieve, like some sort of deranged Energizer Bunny banging the drum until we drop dead one day, about the *last* thing we want to hear is someone telling us, "Oh, just slow down now and rest!"

Well thankyousoverymuch, Barbara! Why didn't I think of that!

For people like me, when we hear that word *rest*, there's a very real part of our brain—a floral-print Draper James–wearing, overly judgy part, perhaps—that thinks you may as well have said "quit" for all it tells us about what you think we're capable of. You don't think we have it in us to go the distance, so we may as well give up right now. I guess we should just sit down here by this lush little stream and take up painting watercolors already. Channel our inner Monet. Maybe we should get a hundred cats. Knit ourselves a Snuggie. Start drinking chamomile tea by the gallon. AND WAIT. FOR DEATH. TO TAKE US.

My judge is also a little dramatic.

But she does get something about me.

Henry David Thoreau spent two years sitting by Walden Pond, at one with nature and pondering this life of quiet desperation. I think I would have lasted a long bank holiday weekend at best.

People like me need something to *do* with our hands.

We want to hear that, even if we aren't out chasing these gold stars and highlight reels for our worth, we will still be able to use this natural drive and ambition to go do work that matters. We need to know that our *life's work* will still matter. When someone says to us, "Give up all this achieving for your worth and lean into rest already," one inevitable question follows.

Then what?

What are we supposed to do with all this *life* that we have left?

GOD,

There is a voice in my head that I have been allowing to speak louder than yours. A voice of judgment telling me that rest is the real enemy.

That voice, Lord, would be happy to watch me work myself to death.

I know that now.

I see it.

God, I don't know how to get free of this voice on my own. I don't know how to heal this deep, damaged place in my brain, but I know it starts by bringing it to you. Asking you how you see it, looking to you to show me what really matters.

God, I can't go on living in survival mode, this primal, visceral fight for my life.

I can't go on chasing two-dimensional paper cutouts of the perfect life.

Show me how to have both rest and purpose.

Show me what to do with all this life that I have left.

AMEN.

SLOW GROWTH PRAYER

№ 20

it's time to heal this wild animal you once became in order to survive

THE WOLF AT LAST COMES HOME

And David said,
"The LORD who
delivered me from the
paw of the lion and
from the paw of the bear
will deliver me from the
hand of this Philistine."
And Saul said to David, "Go,
and the LORD be with you!"

1 SAMUEL 17:37

My running is a girl in a red cape, barefoot and muddy, escaping her way out of the deep, dark woods. Branches clawing at her skin, tearing at her clothes, leaving chunks and pieces of her behind like bread crumbs. Something chasing, always chasing, close behind and closing in fast. The big bad wolf *ripping* at her heels.

She runs because if she stops, she knows it just might kill her.

I am the girl in the red cape.

But when I turn to look back over my shoulder, breathless and wild eyed, I see it.

I am also the wolf.

And that voice in my head telling me to run and not stop running—
that it will *never* be safe for me to stop?

That voice is my own.*

I FEEL THE COLD, hard ground pounding beneath my feet, the thuds echoing out a steady drumbeat of survival in my brain, and with every step I take . . . there is pain.

Somewhere along the line, I have learned to run and not stop running. Chasing . . . always chasing. Clawing at something or someone—some version of me up ahead that is always just beyond my grasp. And when the wincing pain that I carry once again gives rise to a roar, I feel that version of me I was born to protect slip further away in the darkness. A flash of red—this chroma of color, a polaroid moving in reverse—lost somewhere in the shadows of the deep, dark woods. And in the wide-open gaping pain of that separation, of once again failing to somehow keep her safe, I hear a wild animal wail rise up from deep within me.

My heart breaks that I have chased her away yet again.

When you realize you are not only the girl in the red cape but also the wolf, at some point you have to be willing to turn around and stare directly into the face of the wild animal you once had to become in order to survive. You have to be willing to reach out your hand—fearful and faltering at first, afraid of the bared teeth and bared wounds come back all at once to bite you. But when you finally lean in close enough, you can see it: there are thorns in these paws that once were wide-open palms. This animal is not dangerous. This animal of yours is hurt. *Wounded.* And it is counting on you to heal it.

For so many of us, this "run and don't stop running, it will never be safe to stop" self-preservation switch got flipped in us when we were

---

*Marantz, *Dirt*, 224.

"AT A CERTAIN POINT, THE BIG BAD WOLF IS NOW *afraid* OF US."

little, especially if we didn't grow up with a lot. We have spent a lifetime letting the wolf chase us. Because at least if we were running, we didn't have to stay where we were.

We *used* that adrenaline. We became addicted to it. We feared we would forget how to move forward altogether if we didn't have something constantly clawing at our heels. The greatest fear for those of us who are trying to break free from all this achieving for our worth is this right here: What if I do the work to get healed and in doing so, I lose all my drive?*

What if I lose my edge? What if I suddenly have to be content being ordinary . . . average? What if I stop winning, stop being the girl who always comes through, and in doing so I just disappear altogether?

So we go from the one being chased to the one twisting the thorn.

We cage that wild animal within us, lock it up in captivity, make it dance in our three-ring circus show. One where we *always* get to be the high-wire act.

And when it won't perform like we want it to, we press our thumbs into these wide-open wounds. We know all the best pressure points to hit, we know just the right raw nerve endings to expose, in order to make this animal go roaring back into fight-or-flight mode anytime we need it. Just enough pain to keep it running, but never so much that it collapses altogether.

If we can't stop, that means the wolf can't either.

So we allow it to go on wailing, limping behind us in pain. Because the girl in the red cape doesn't know who she is without the big bad wolf ripping at her heels. And figuring out how to stand on her own without him?

*I first began thinking about this idea from a conversation with Knox McCoy in episode 49 of *The Mary Marantz Show* about his book *All Things Reconsidered* (Nashville: Thomas Nelson, 2020).

Well, that becomes the scariest pursuit of all.

If we want to have the slightest chance of breaking free from this achieving and letting go of all this "not enough" still hanging over our heads, here is our way forward. We have to recognize that at a certain point, *we* become the dangerous ones. At a certain point, the big bad wolf is now afraid of *us*. This trail of bread crumbs made from all the different pieces of us has finally led our way back home. And emerging from the shadows of a stark, frozen landscape we once knew is the face of a wild animal that is also our own. Its pained eyes are the reflection we finally see once we are ready to stand face-to-face and deal with all the shattered pieces of this mirror. When the wolf wails out in agony from a lifetime spent proving, doubled over there at the pain, we now notice that it is *our* throats that are raw from all the roaring. When we twist the thorn in his paw and dig in a little deeper, torturing him just to keep him running, we now notice that *our* palms are the ones that are bleeding.

We are the wolf. And we are the girl who has spent a lifetime running.

And if it's time now to stop, then *we* have to stop being our own captors.

It's time to set this wild thing free.

GOD,

I am tired of all this chasing. Me chasing after other people. Chasing all these other versions of me I thought I had to become in order to belong. The girl in the red cape chasing me. The big bad wolf chasing her.

We spend our whole lives running, never once turning around to really see one another.

When I think about what true rest looks like to me now, I imagine the grown-up me, the little me, and the wolf all together somewhere in green pastures. We have been led there to safety. We lie down beside still waters.

We're at peace now. We're playing.

We're there with you, God. And you love us all the same.

Every version of us we once had to become in order to survive. Every version of us we will one day be. You look on each of us, and at once we are seen, we are known, and we are deeply loved.

You shine your healing light into every still-open wound.

We are held there, safe in your hands.

And from a deep place inside that we all somehow recognize at once, we know that this is what it looks like to be set free.

AMEN.

anchoring

HO

PART III

PE

*slow growth equals
strong roots*

21

where once there was chasing apparel, parallels chasing apparel, now true rest begins to take root

RUNNING
OR ROOTED?

They will be like a tree
planted by the water that sends
out its roots by the stream. It
does not fear when heat comes;
its leaves are always green.
It has no worries in a year of
drought and never fails to bear fruit.

JEREMIAH 17:8 NIV

IF YOU RUN from your story long enough, sooner or later you are going to find yourself at a place in the road where you thought you would be further along by now.

It will begin with the appearance of tiny mile markers tucked just off to the side of the path, barely even visible for having gotten lost somewhere in the overgrown weeds. But as you tread along, the sound of your own two feet striking pay dirt and thudding out a heavy heartbeat of *Evermore* in your head, the signs all around you begin to get bigger. They start counting down to something, like those giant billboards in the Carolinas telling you it's only 150 more miles until the next must-do attraction. You can feel the urgency rising up inside of you now, though you're not really sure why.

All you know is that you only have so many more miles to go before you need to accomplish *everything* you once set out to do.

At a certain point, maybe you stop moving forward. You double over there on the side of the well-beaten path—these dug-in ruts and rules of the road oft traveled. You steady yourself with your hands on your knees, head bowed low in a posture of prayer, while you try to remind yourself what it feels like to breathe. Maybe you even go ahead and sit down there on the sidelines for a while, rest in the shadow of an old oak tree. The soft sage grass brushing against the backs of your legs beckons you, whispers to you on a gentle breeze, quietly inviting you to stay there for a little while longer.

And for one brief minute of reprieve, you forget what all this running was for.

But while you are stopped there beside lush streams in green pastures, you can't help noticing that no one else has dropped out of the race like you thought they would. No one has joined you in this new, noble pursuit of rest. In fact, they haven't even once broken their stride. Now you've not only been lapped by the hare . . . but that holier-than-thou tortoise too. It turns out, slow and steady doesn't change a thing if all you still care about is winning.

In a world full of gold stars and these gold-medal runners constantly outpacing you, all with Olympic-sized ambitions, you realize that part of your struggle with rest all along has been not wanting to be left behind. If we could all somehow just agree to bow out of this rat race together in solidarity, all sit down at the very same time on the count of three, it feels like it would be easier. Instead, these runners blow by you in a dead heat, pushing past one another to be first, ever addicted to the endorphins, always chasing the next high, their finger forever on the pulse of what it takes to win.

You have now come to resent the runners as much as you resent the race. And as they go by, you could swear you could see from somewhere out of the corner of their side eye—this rapid "me, myself, and I" movement—that to them *you* are what it now looks like to quit.

This is your crossroads moment.

And now you have to decide.

Are you going to be a person who cares more about winning races or growing strong roots?

"A LIFE SPENT STANDING in one place on the shore, becoming a tree, honestly sounds pretty boring to me. It sounds like quitting."

I say these words to Coach Kim as she resumes her place at my white kitchen island. She's in town for our annual goal-setting retreat, and I'm telling her how I'm supposed to be writing this whole book on the virtue of strong roots. All the while there's this huge part of me that can't stop thinking of them as shackles.

One of my favorite scriptures is from the book of Jeremiah: "They will be like a tree planted by the water that sends out its roots by the stream. It does not fear when heat comes; its leaves are always green. It has no worries in a year of drought and never fails to bear fruit" (Jer. 17:8 NIV).

I love this verse. When I read it, it makes me think once again of the vine and the branches. It makes me think about being tapped into this life source that is never-ending. It makes me think about a true oasis in the middle of the dry, scorched-earth desert and how I'll never have to be thirsty again.

But I have to be honest here.

When I first think about becoming a tree, all I can think about is being *stuck*.

Just when you begin to get

ROOTED

you try to break loose to run free once again.

The mud draws up all around my ankles, fast like quicksand. A tangle of hands and roots then bursts forth from the ground, clawing at my Achilles' heels, intertwining with the sinew of every muscle until my legs feel heavy, like they are no longer my own. Before I know it, I'm twelve inches deep in this shallow grave. It is a monument to a life that up until now I have lived entirely for myself, and it is at last coming to an end. But rather than resting there in the peace of what's coming, there is one last resurrected rush of self-sufficiency. A gnawing and thrashing of the will. Just when you begin to get rooted, you try to break loose to run free once again.

In a lot of ways, becoming a tree still feels like quitting to me.

It's like you weren't cut out for the race, you didn't have it in you to win. So you just sat down here on this hill to die on and decided to never move again.

This at first appears to be the tension of life: we are either running for our worth, breathless and exhausted, forever coming in last place in a race we never signed up for. Or we sit down one day and decide to stay stuck. We plant our flag, and in doing so we commit to staying put, to forfeiting every finish line we could have ever gone on to chase. We decide to just become this one thing that stays in one place and bears one kind of fruit for the rest of our lives until we die.

I imagine this rooted life in my mind, every day looking out at the same horizon. The same sunrises, the same sunsets. Watching my life stand still while all around people are running past me in a blur. I have become someone who is no longer moving forward. Someone who will never know if she even had it in her to win the race because she gave up before it was over.

Kim takes this all in, the way she always does. She picks all the icing off of one blueberry pancake cupcake, which we got her as a surprise from Sugar, a favorite local bakery of ours. She scoops it all off with one finger and sets it to the side while I look on, mildly horrified.

I feel like she's missing the best part. But true to form, Kim is only interested in getting down to the real stuff, to the crumbly center underneath all that extra icing the world loves to layer on.

"Y'know," she says in between blueberry bites, "if all we're ever doing is fighting the crowd for that next sunny spot on the shore, forever racing from place to place looking for our next moment in the spotlight, we're going to find ourselves spending most of our life in darkness. Spending most of our life being left out in the cold."

At this, I think about what some of my starkest seasons of striving have felt like. "Dark and cold" seems pretty accurate.

Kim pauses, tracing the outline of a now empty cupcake wrapper as she searches for the right words, all the crumbs I've been chasing for a lifetime spilled out on the counter between us.

She nods her head at something. She has decided. She now knows what needs to be said.

"Whereas if we'll just stand firm in our place on the shore, digging in to what we were created for, growing for something other than ourselves, if we stand there long enough . . . the light has a funny way of finding us."

Rooted or running?

We get to decide.

GOD,

I thank you for all the ways you are helping me put down roots. Not just for a season of staying in one place, but for these good virtues you are growing in me while I wait.

Thank you that you plant us beside cool streams, this gentle salve to the wound that is healing us while we rest.

Lord, I praise you for how you protect us in the drought. And that where the world's economy says this looks like quitting, you in your beautiful provision determine that we will not cease to bear good fruit.

Thank you that we are never in a race with other people, we are never late to our own lives.

You are slowing us down so that we can grow strong roots.

What a gift it is to grow according to your plan.

AMEN.

№ 22

22

WEED, FLOWER, TREE

where once there was comparison, now purpose begins to take root

For each tree is known by its own fruit. For figs are not gathered from thornbushes, nor are grapes picked from a bramble bush.

LUKE 6:44

THIS IS FOR THE ONE who is tired right now, bone weary and ready to give up.

I want to remind you today, all we are asked to do is be faithful with the planting.

We can tend, we can water. We can wait, we can watch. We can stare with hopeful eyes at the cold, hard ground for any signs of change emerging from the darkness. A new thing growing wild in the wilderness, these too often despised days of small beginnings that burst forth when you least expect it and turn their brave, brand-new faces for the very first time to feel the warmth of the sun. And when the light hits just right you'll know.

You were always the one asked to be faithful with the planting.

But you were *never* the one with the power to make it grow.

The other day I was talking to Justin about all these dreams we hold in our hands. I told him through salty, hopeful tears, "We can plant the seeds in the ground, but we can't go in and rip them open in the hopes of speeding up the process."

If you really pause to think about it, there is magic there. Miracle.

You can be the best gardener in the world. All the conditions can be right. The best tools. All the right know-how. A fertile ground to start from. But no matter what you do, you cannot force a thing to grow.

Somewhere between the planting and the harvest, we have to leave room for the miracle to happen. This magic that occurs in darkness, away from the watchful eyes of a waiting world. Those moments when you think you are buried, but that's really when the most important work is being done.

That's when you realize, it was never up to you to make it happen.

And there is freedom there. True rest.

For the past several years, I've been working on this very scientific theory that when it comes to our life's work, there are basically three types of people we can choose to be: weeds, flowers, or trees.

WEEDS. Weeds are very successful at first glance. They seem to pop up out of nowhere overnight and grow faster than everyone else around them. Their presence spreads like wildfire. Where one day there was nothing, suddenly the next day they are everywhere you turn. And as their reach grows to dizzying heights almost instantly, it is *very* tempting to say that you want to grow just like a weed. That is, until you realize that in the weed's insatiable desire to grow upward,

"WE CAN PLANT THE *seeds* IN THE GROUND, BUT WE CAN'T GO IN AND RIP THEM OPEN IN THE HOPES OF SPEEDING UP THE *process*."

higher and higher, heads above the rest . . . they have forgotten to grow deep. They have spent so much of their energy on how big and impressive they are on the surface that they never got around to making sure they also had roots. Something of substance and surety they are anchored to. And what that means for them is that when the slightest storm comes, the slightest push, they fall right over. Who among us has not pulled out a five-foot weed with the slightest effort, only to discover it was standing on barely a couple inches of roots? They grew only for themselves. They stood for nothing. They took instead of giving. And that, it turns out, will always be their undoing. They are but a flash in the pan. They fall away as quickly as they once rose.

FLOWERS. Flowers provide a very important service in the world, to be sure. They are the purveyors of beauty. And goodness knows the world certainly needs more beauty. In terms of their life's work, there are flowers who are annuals. These are the kinds of people who create something really pretty, beautiful even, and it flourishes for a season and then it's gone. Then there is the good work that is perennial. These people know the kind of beauty that they were born to create, they own it, and they are able to deliver on that year after year. On its face, there is nothing wrong with being merely a flower in your work. Beauty is, in and of itself, a gift to the world. And so is building a beautiful life. But for all of us, I want something *more*.

TREES. And then you have those people who go beyond just growing for themselves, who go beyond just making something pretty. Those people are what I call trees. See, a tree can grow up and up, as high as you can imagine, with its arms stretched out wide. But here's the interesting thing about a tree that you might not know: for however high and wide a tree stretches its branches . . . its roots will always stretch wider. It digs in before it ever tries to grow up. And as a result,

> *MY HOPE IS THAT WE WILL ALWAYS STRIVE TO BE TREES. TO GROW AND STRETCH OUR FINGERS TOWARD THE SKY, BUT NEVER OUT OF REACH OF OUR ROOTS AND WHERE WE CAME FROM.*

it is not tossed by every storm that comes. It knows what it stands for, it holds fast to what it's anchored to. And while a tree may indeed be a thing of incredible beauty, it is never satisfied with being merely that. Instead, it chooses to also bear fruit. To create something to be shared and given away so that others might be fed by what it has created.

In all of our lives, my hope is that we will always strive to be trees. To grow and stretch our fingers toward the sky, but never out of reach of our roots and where we came from. To provide shade and shelter for others. To be not just a thing of beauty that fades but something that leaves others better for having found us. And to choose to grow slow and steady over the long haul, because that's how you get to walk among the giants.

And anytime that growing gets just a little too slow, I hope we will remind ourselves of what Justin is always telling me, what he has been telling me patiently for the last fifteen years . . .

Slow growth equals strong roots.

Here's to the trees of the world. May you always stand strong.

SLOW GROWTH PRAYER

GOD,

Thank you for how you invite us to grow for something bigger than ourselves. Thank you that you allow us to be part of this legacy of giving.

We know that every time we cast our eyes on something bigger, on this abundance that can be given away, you are setting us free—shackle by shackle—from these chains of achieving and a life lived only for ourselves.

Lord, I thank you that you knew my story from the very beginning. You were so involved in the process of my becoming that you planted an entire field of weeds behind our trailer. So that I would always remember how easy they are to uproot. How being an overnight success means nothing if you can be knocked down by the very first push.

And thank you for placing me in a family that knew all about trees, this growing with character and integrity over the long haul.

Weeds and trees, Lord. I have witnessed both.

And I am grateful for the chance to stand strong.

AMEN.

23

WHEN GROWING
SLOW IS THE WORST

where once there was impatience,
now character begins to take root

But they who wait for the LORD
shall renew their strength; they shall
mount up with wings like eagles;
they shall run and not be weary;
they shall walk and not grow faint.

ISAIAH 40:31

IF WE'RE GOING to be serious about this *Slow Growth Equals Strong Roots* journey, we're going to have to get really honest right here about this one unfortunate part.

Ready?

Sometimes growing slow is the absolute *worst*.

At least it can feel that way when you're in the thickest part of the weeds and everyone else around you is succeeding overnight.

It hits the hardest in those moments when you feel it right in your chest, like a frustrated freight train of pent-up energy trying to burst forth out of you into the world. Next thing you know, every muscle in your body is flexed and your neck is in full-on traction. Now you're nothing but stretched tendons, clenched jaws turned clenched fists, this pressure-cooker pulse that's pressed so tight against your skin you swear you can see it beating there just below the surface. Your head pounds. Your teeth grind to a screeching halt. You are practically vibrating with the unfairness of it all, oscillating somewhere between a pity party of one and raging against the machine.

Why is it always so easy for everyone else?

It makes me think about the word *angst* (noun), "a feeling of deep anxiety, worry or dread, typically set off by something trivial."*

If my slow growth angst were a person, it would definitely wear flannel. Its hair would be long and stringy. It would probably live in Seattle and smell like Teen Spirit. Nevermind that it could be found most days banging its head against a wall.

Nobody likes growing slow when they're right in the middle of it.

Most of us are walking around like the Ricky Bobby of our own lives: *We wanna go fast.* We wanna win races. We feel like if we ain't first, we're last. And when it seems like nothing is happening the way we want it to, *we don't know what to do with our HANDS.*

I once had a sinus infection—the worst one I ever had. It felt like an entire pillowcase of stuffing had been packed up my nose. It felt like someone was doing an actual handstand on my face with their thumbs digging directly into my cheekbones, the full weight of their body pressing down on me. It felt like a geyser of pressure was going to explode right out of my forehead any minute and rain down in a confetti of Kleenex and Sudafed.

And *then* I got on an airplane.

That's how it feels when slow growth hurts.

You're blocked up. You don't know how to breathe. It feels like the weight of the world is pushing down on you. And *then* you add cabin pressure.

Oxford Languages, s.v. "angst," accessed June 21, 2021, https://www.lexico.com/en/definition /angst.

In those moments when everyone is moving faster than we are, when we feel like we've already been lapped in last place, when it's happening for everyone but us and everyone else is getting their turn in the winner's circle . . . what do we cling to for hope that this doesn't ultimately disqualify us from the race?

Can I be really honest here? We're tired.

We're tired of doing the right things. We're tired of showing up and showing up and showing up some more. We're tired of doing the work. We're tired of sowing the seeds and having nothing yet to show for it. We're tired of the tending. We're tired of the watchful waiting, this wait and see approach we seem to be taking to the whole rest of our lives.

We have grown weary of our own bootstraps. We have pulled ourselves back up one too many times. We're tired of the pep talks we have to give ourselves over and over about how our breakthrough is just around the corner, pep talks we don't even believe anymore, this white noise filling the void. We feel like we're *lying* in wait. Praying for a moment that never comes.

Deep breath.

God *knew* the waiting would be hard.

That's why he mentions that word *wait* 89 times in the Bible. He even knew this growing slow while everyone else is moving fast all around us would be hard. Especially when it feels like those people are cutting corners to get there. Look at what he tells us: "Be still before the Lord and wait patiently for him; fret not yourself over the one who prospers in his way" (Ps. 37:7).

Fret not. If only it were that easy.

But God isn't surprised by this either. So he also reminds us, "Let us not grow weary of doing good, for in due season we will reap, if we do not give up" (Gal. 6:9).

I don't know about you, but I think I would have been a pretty terrible farmer. You would find me out there stomping around in the field, veins protruding from my sun-scorched neck, shaking clenched fists at the sky and cursing the ground for having the audacity to be made of real, actual dirt instead of some fabricated, synthetic Miracle-Gro mulch turned overly fertile ground.

Good things take time to grow. *Real* things take time to grow.

But try telling that to someone with a freight train of possibility about to burst right out of her chest.

Believe it or not, God knew that was coming too. So in his infinite wisdom, he gives us a scripture to cling to that I believe even Ricky Bobby himself could get on board with: "But they who wait for the LORD shall renew their strength; they shall mount up with wings like eagles; they shall run and not be weary; they shall walk and not grow faint" (Isa. 40:31).

Repeat those words over and over to yourself when the slow growing gets hard. Heck, put on Whitesnake's "Here I Go Again on My Own" if you have to. But crank that power ballad up in your heart. *Oh Lord, I pray you give us strength to carry on.*

God has made you a slow-growing *warrior.* And when faced with the choice between growing slow and doing it the right way, this building integrity and character over the long haul, or cutting corners just to get ahead . . . we already know the answer he has written on our hearts.

And we *will not* grow weary of doing good.

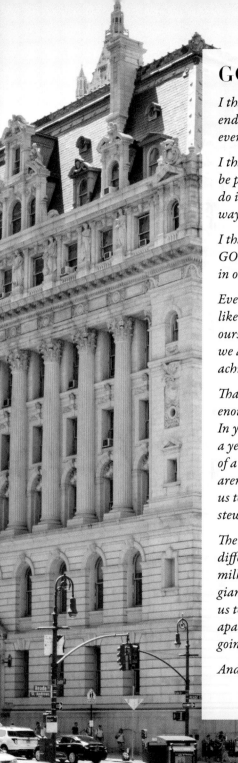

GOD,

I thank you for this character and this endurance that you are growing in us every time the answer is "not yet."

I thank you that you have called us to be people of integrity, who would rather do it the right way than merely the fast way.

I thank you that you are growing GOOD things and REAL things not only in our lives but in our hearts as well.

Every time this slow growth feels like it's taking too long, we remind ourselves—it is far more important who we are becoming than anything we are achieving.

Thank you that you care about us enough to sometimes slow things down. In your infinite wisdom, you know when a yes or a sudden success would be more of a burden than a blessing because we aren't ready for it yet. You are preparing us to be the kind of person who can steward something like that well.

There is a reason you came up with a different timeline for how long it takes milkweed to grow than a redwood giant. When the growing gets slow, help us to remember that you have set us apart. Weeds may grow fast. But we are going to get to walk among the giants.

And that kind of growth takes time.

AMEN.

SLOW GROWTH PRAYER

№ 24

where once there was insatiable, now a servant heart begins to take root

A VERUCA SALT–WORTHY TANTRUM

*For what shall it profit a man,
if he shall gain the whole
world, and lose his own soul?*

MARK 8:36 KJV

ONE OF MY FAVORITE country songs has this line talking about how we need to focus less on what's next and more on what's right now.

I love that line and I hate that line. Because the truth is, I have always been a "what's next" kind of girl.

A few years into the photography business I owned with my husband, Justin, I started an annual tradition of looking back every December and answering three questions: What worked? What didn't? and What's next? I started blogging my answers. And eventually the whole thing turned into an in-person workshop we hosted for other business owners and then a cross-country speaking tour complete with a rented tour bus that had our faces printed larger than life on the side.

(Side note: If you have never showered in bumper-to-bumper traffic while going through the Lincoln Tunnel, I don't highly recommend it.)

If "What's Next" were a person, I think she would look just like Veruca Salt from the movie *Willy Wonka and the Chocolate Factory*. All buttoned up in her little red pinafore dress with the white Peter Pan collar and matching tights, stomping her little Mary Jane–clad foot, purple-faced and hollering, "I want the goose that laid the golden egg, Daddy, and I want it *now*! Gooses! Geeses!"*

She would have that same deranged look in her eye. That same frizzy-yet-somehow-stringy hair falling in front of her face—this unhinged mixture of Jessie Spano when she's so excited that she's somehow scared and Rob Zombie's 2007 take on Michael Myers. The look of a girl who has gotten everything she's ever wanted, seen it all come true one by one, only to get to the end and still never be satisfied that it's enough. In frustration, What's Next would knock over all the candy bowls and kick all the pretty wrapped boxes, these beautiful gifts that were always meant for someone else. She would unravel all the cellophane and generally leave a path of mess and destruction in her wake.

In the movie, Veruca sing-speaks some of the most selfish words anyone could say, and I have to tell you, I feel pretty personally attacked by them. She tells us how she wants the world—the *whole* world. And not only that. She wants to lock it away in her pocket so no one else can ever have it. She wants to have her chocolate bar and eat it too.

What's Next is somehow an exercise in both scarcity and gluttony at the very same time. An insatiable appetite for the next sugary-sweet

---

Willy Wonka and the Chocolate Factory, directed by Mel Stuart (Warner Bros., 1971).

high that is born out of a deep, aching hunger. It is this incessant desire to get everything you ever wanted . . . and to lock it away so no one else can have it. So no one else can ever take it from you again.

It is also this utter lack of concern for *how* wrapped up in pursuit of the far more interesting, far more flavorful *now*. As What's Next is always quick to remind us, "Doesn't matter how, I want it now!" But as Coach Kim tells me often when we're working together on setting some new goal, what we are *getting* in pursuit of these achievements is far less interesting than who we are *becoming*.

Here's a revelation I had recently: God is a master of both the infinite and the instant . . . who somehow fell in love with the *process*.

Think about it. Here's God, who could have ten separate universes spinning at the end of every one of his fingertips at the mere whisper of a word, every axis trembling at his touch. And yet, he spends his days helping me become just a little less selfish. Just a little less envious. Just a little less wrapped up in things that don't ultimately matter.

Here is God, who could spend his days basking in his own *phenomenal cosmic power in this itty-bitty living space* we call Earth. But instead he chooses to spend his days as the potter, spinning the wheel. Working and reworking the clay of my heart. Every day he's there, reshaping my character to be just a little closer to the version of me he always had in mind. This God who has infinite *now* power somehow fell in love with the *how*. With this *process* over time.

And I guess that's the picture of What's Right Now.

If What's Next is stomping her feet and running around, screaming out her list of demands, What's Right Now is the clay, content to be held there in the Father's hands. Hopeful for what she will one day become. Grateful for the opportunity to be changed and molded, for another day to get one step closer to the version of herself she was always meant to be. Knowing with all certainty that she was created on

This God who has infinite

now

POWER

somehow fell in love with the

how.

purpose for a purpose. Faithful that she will get there on time when God says the moment is right.

And when she does get there, she won't lock it all away from the rest of the world, storing up all the gifts and surprises along the way for herself. Instead, What's Right Now will take the shape of a pitcher, pouring it all out for others. Thankful that God made her into something that can be filled up over and over again. A vessel designed by him, forever operating out of the overflow.

If you've never seen *Willy Wonka and the Chocolate Factory*, here's a spoiler alert for you. At the end of Veruca Salt's self-serving temper tantrum, she finds herself standing on a scale where she is quickly judged to be a bad egg. So she is immediately tossed out. Thrown out with the garbage. Most likely headed to the furnace, we're told.

Thank God we don't live in a Wonka economy like that. Thank God that where the rest of the world would be so quick to throw us away, God leans in to our temper-tantrum moments—those times when we want it now and we don't care how and we only want it all for ourselves. He sees it all and loves us anyway.

He invites us to something better.

But first he loves us, kicking and screaming right where we are.

GOD,

I thank you that you are making vessels where once we only held vanity and empty-calorie ambition.

The truth is, I have been my own version of Veruca Salt far more times than I would ever want to admit. The temper tantrums I have thrown in private, the times when I have wished all the perfectly wrapped gifts were my own—I am so thankful that the world wasn't there to witness those.

There have been so many times when I wanted to keep it all for myself, God. Lock every good thing away so that no one else could take it from me. But every day, you are reminding me that if we want to get out of our own heads, out of our own prison of perfection, we do that by serving others.

God, what a gift it is to be molded by you. Not only are you making me a better, truer version of myself, but you are also making me into something useful. Someone who can pour out the gifts she has been given in service to others.

AMEN.

where once there was control, now gratitude and faith begin to take root

WE ALL HAVE A MISSING SQUARE

Why, even
the hairs of
your head are
all numbered.
Fear not; you
are of more value
than many sparrows.

LUKE 12:7

EVERY SINGLE ONE of us has a missing square.

We all have that one social media post we wish we were making, a highlight moment missing in our day-to-day lives that leaves us reeling, a caption that has remained written out word for word in our minds that we've never once been able to push publish on.

I don't know if for you that square looks like a job announcement, a post declaring "I'm going back to school to get that degree," a bought-my-first-house or building-my-dream-home hashtag, or a carousel of photos of you getting engaged on the edge of a cliff-hanger where the answer is always yes.

But the point is, all of us are waiting for something.

For me, that missing square has looked like two pink lines on a plastic stick. An ultrasound photo styled with one of those letter boards and a coming soon date. A Christmas card photo with a new addition.

Every year for the last few years we have taken our Christmas card photo on our front porch. It has become our tradition. And there's just something about taking it in the same place every year that allows all the changes that have come and gone in our lives to shine even brighter. We have added puppies and lost older dogs we've loved for a lifetime. We've gone from two dogs down to one dog, back to two, up to three, and then back down to only two again. That's a lot of love and loss in the space of a few years. We have had the porch redone and added in the beautiful stone steps I dreamed of for ten years before we ever got around to doing it. And just last year we were able to include *Dirt* tied up with a little red ribbon in the corner of the photo.

But for however much our annual photo allows what's new to shine, it has also had the glaring effect of highlighting what isn't. We still don't have a family. I can't tell you how many times I've felt frozen in time looking at those photos. Same porch, same red bows, same wreath, same childhood sled, generally the same sort of outfits. Year after year goes by and there we sit, no baby to report.

And every year I share our card, I feel like the whole world is watching us and thinking the very same thing: *Man, those guys are still missing something.*

There is a pretty lettered sign I keep in our bedroom on the wall right by our bed. It says, "You, me, and the dogs." It is both beautiful and heartbreaking all at the same time. An inspiration and an indictment. On the one hand, it reminds me of what really matters in our life. Of what would be the first thing we would save if there was ever a fire. All we really need to survive.

But it is also a daily reminder of what is missing.

And every year that goes by where we can't share that square, it gets a little harder to believe this truth that God still has good things for

us. A plan for us. To prosper us and not to harm us. To give us hope and a future.

If there's one thing I know about overachievers it's this: we have an *idea* of how things are supposed to go. A picture in our heads of what the "good life" looks like. And for most of us, we've always been able to push and perform, do the work, show up, show up some more, show no mercy, control the situation. And by sheer force of grit and tenacity mixed with some good old-fashioned persistence, we've always been able to get the outcome we desire.

Except that one square.

That one square that's still missing reminds us that we're not really in control. There is no amount of striving that can force it to be. This good life we've been building is not guaranteed. We can get the job and get the house and even get the white kitchen island. We can check every other box on our list and still feel like our whole world is missing.

Ninety-nine dreams that have been a lifetime in the making can come true all around us in big, bright, blinking, neon-sign fashion.

And still we will go looking for the one.

In a lot of ways, it's felt like running a marathon only to get to the end and find out that the race has been canceled. Or maybe more to the point, that everyone else has already finished and gone home. The organizers have packed up and left. The folding tables have been put away. There are only empty paper water cups where the finish line should be.

And here we are, still just trying to arrive.

These missing moments, these missing squares—God is using them to show me that following him isn't about getting everything I ever wanted exactly how and when I thought I would. He's teaching me that if I could steamroll every element of my so-called good life into fruition through my own sheer force of will, then I would miss out on the better plans he has for me. He's showing me that rarely do we ever get to go through life with every box checked exactly the way we think it should be. And yet, we still have to find a way to fall in love with our hard, messy, broken, beautiful lives anyway, right in this moment, right here and now . . . while we're still living them.

Even if the answer is still no.

Life isn't about checking every box. It isn't about filling every square. When we trust God, we trust the blank spaces.

And until he sees fit to change it, "You, me, and the dogs" is still a pretty good life.

I'VE BEEN PRAYING for a daughter of my own for the last nearly eight years. For the first few years, I spent all my time praying for a *daughter.* Then, when that didn't work out, I started praying *for* my daughter.

It's a subtle distinction that, as it turns out, changes everything. One involves me telling God what I want, what I need, how I think it should go. The other is about me praying out of faith for what I believe will one day be, even when I can't see a way forward. If I believe God is in the business of fulfilling his promises (which I do), and if I believe that he's placed a promise of a daughter in my heart in the shape of this picture in my head I just can't shake, then what I know for certain is that I don't want my daughter to arrive, however that may happen, and for that to be the first day I have ever prayed for her.

The day I finally hold her in my arms, I want to be able to whisper, "I have prayed for you a thousand times before, and I will pray at least a million more."

For most of my life, I believed that I was going to go out and be the break in some pretty heavy generational chains. I believed that because of the work I was doing with my life, *my* kids would one day have it easier. For years, that good life looked to me like a warm, beautiful, well-decorated home. It was money in the bank. Beach vacations. The good jeans when it was time to go school shopping. An SUV for the drop-off line.

Now, though, when I pray *for* my daughter, what I hope more than anything for her is this: I hope she knows how deeply, intimately, unconditionally loved and known she is from the moment she wakes up. I hope she knows there isn't a thing she can do or accomplish that will make me love her more. And there isn't a mistake she can make that can separate her from that love.

I hope she knows that when she sleeps, I'll be there counting the hairs on her head. In wonderstruck awe at every last one. I hope she knows that I'll see every one of her fingerprints as nothing short of a miracle, these whorls and ridges that carve out a path that belongs only to her. One that she alone can walk. I hope she knows she can come to me and lay everything before me, big or small.

I pray she knows that when she's in pain, I too will be in pain. When she weeps and mourns and suffers, I'll weep and mourn and suffer right alongside her. And I'll willingly take every bit of that heavy burden from her that she'll allow me to carry. I pray she knows that when she celebrates, there will be no one prouder than me. I will hang the very stars themselves in the sky like a canvas of confetti, blinking in and out of her existence, paled by the light she gives off.

I will draw down close to her every chance I get. Breathe in this little life so full of big possibilities. Feel the heart in my very own chest start to hammer out a bass line until it's keeping time with the beat of her own drum. A backbeat, driving rhythm thudding out this promised melody: "There is nothing you're not worthy of."

I will whisper over her with every breath I have that there is no amount of achieving, performing, striving—no combination of gold stars and the right boxes checked—that will ever make me love her more than I do right now, right here, today.

And then I think, if I can feel this way about my someday, hoped-for daughter . . .

How much more does God feel that for *his* own daughters right now?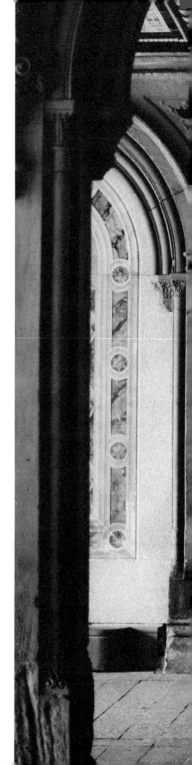

GOD,

I want to trade this conditional worship I have had for you, for an "Even if . . ." kind of love.

Even if we never get that one square, God, I choose you.

Even if the answer is never yes, I trust you.

Even if my heart is currently breaking, I choose to believe that you have something better.

I might not be able to see it right now, Lord, but I do have hope in who you say you are.

Thank you for the care you take with each of our stories.

Thank you for the shift you have already made in my heart from praying to get what I want to praying in faith for your plans that are always better than my own.

With every day that you work on my heart, I know you are shaping me to be the kind of mother I always dreamed of being. That's the kind of change that is going to have generational impact.

And I trust that good things like that take time.

AMEN.

№

26

OPEN YOUR HAND

where once there was entitlement and attachment; now surrender begins to take root

But godliness with contentment is great gain, for we brought nothing into the world, and we cannot take anything out of the world.

1 TIMOTHY 6:6–7

TWO MORE THINGS we are going to have to give up if we're going to chase a life that's on fire with purpose and led by God are as follows: entitlement and attachment.

Entitlement is that little voice that whispers "that should be yours." It could be hissing in your ear in the form of comparison, asking you why someone else is getting everything you ever wanted—someone who is clearly less qualified, has not worked as hard, and is not nearly as nice as you. Or perhaps it puts on the disguise of a carousel ad on Facebook, showing you every pretty sweater and pair of shoes you could ever possibly want, until your head is spinning—this merry-go-round of more—with all the things you do not yet have.

Maybe it's someone else's milestone achievement, a throw-the-confetti mountaintop moment that was *years* in the climb. Maybe they just paid off all their debt, launched their business, or wrote a book like

217

you've always dreamed of. Maybe they finished that degree you never started. Or applied for that opportunity you never hit send on.

Maybe it's a dream in your heart, and you feel like God *owes* you. After all, the Bible says, "Delight yourself in the LORD, and he will give you the desires of your heart" (Ps. 37:4). *I'm ready, God. Here's my Amazon wishlist.* And every unanswered prayer feels like a personal affront to everything you hold dear.

You start to tell yourself a cacophony of silent alarms and prewritten scripts about how much *easier* it was for them. How this hard story disqualifies you, like some forged permission slip for seventh grade gym class that allows you to sit this one out. "Please excuse Mary from her entire life. She didn't always have the easiest story growing up."

So often we get caught up in this idea that So&So (a subsidiary of If I Could Only Be Like Them, Inc.) did it this way. Step-by-step, this was their path to success. And if I'll just place my feet carefully in their footsteps, never once overstepping the outer edges of their size 8 marks on the world, then I too can get to wherever it is they've gotten.

And the faster, the better.

But here's the thing about feeling entitled to someone else's path: it means you're never once blazing your own trail. And here's the thing about holding on so tightly to someone else's version of success: you have no idea how much you might be shortchanging what it is you're actually capable of. And day after day you go on, trading in your "go out and leave this world a better place" for their "hey, it looks pretty on the internet."

Entitlement is going to tell you that it should be yours, not theirs. How it should be easy. It will whisper how other people owe you something when it comes to opening doors to your success.

Attachment, on the other hand, is like the warm, worn security blanket we hold on to so tightly in our balled-up fists. It's Linus and his ever-present blue companion in the Charlie Brown movies. It's these woven threads turned twenty-pound weights that we can't bring ourselves to lay down.

When I was little, my security blanket was actually a little blue gingham robe lined with quilt backing on the inside that I called "ba-ba." I took it with me everywhere, held it in my tiny hands, until the quilted liner was worn down to nothing more than threadbare blue squares. And when disaster inevitably struck and I left it behind somewhere—or it got thrown out because there was not much left of it at all—a new security blanket would inevitably appear.

Not much has changed for me as a grown-up.

I have these attachments to how things are *supposed* to go that I carry around with me in my tightly clenched hands. I take them with me everywhere I go until they are worn and threadbare, these see-through cloaks that can no longer provide comfort. And when I have used them up, worn them down to nothing, a new one will inevitably appear to take its place.

We become attached to the outcome. We become attached to the pro forma in which the promise is delivered. We become attached to the season finale story lines that we write in our own heads about how our lives should turn out.

"Give me the pen, God. I can write this better than you can."

The very first time I stood on a stage and shared with the audience that Justin and I were having trouble starting a family, I was already writing the Shonda Rhimes–worthy cliff-hanger in my head. This season might end with me standing alone on a stage. But I just knew in my heart that the very next year I would walk out from behind the curtains with a baby in my arms or, at the very least, with a giant belly leading the way.

That didn't happen.

And it didn't happen the year after that or the year after that.

I had an attachment in my head to how I thought the story was sup-posed to go. I felt entitled to get the yes I prayed so hard for—even more so with every passing pregnancy announcement, ultrasound photo, and

When we trust the Author, we trust the

STORY.

perfectly styled baby shower I saw on Instagram. I felt attached to this promise and entitled to the outcome because I felt like everything about the hard parts of my story would only serve to make me a better mom.

And yet, I stood on stage alone.

This past Christmas, I saw someone share a post about Linus and his little blue blanket. It said that the only time we ever see Linus drop his blanket in the entire history of the *Peanuts* comic is in *A Charlie Brown Christmas* when he shares "what Christmas is all about."

He is alone on stage.

There is a spotlight on his every move. And right at the moment he utters the words "Fear not!" he finally drops his security blanket. Attachment falls away. Entitlement doesn't seem to matter anymore.

You know the thing about holding on too tight? Gripping a dream with both hands, arms shaking, choking the life out of what made that dream beautiful in the first place, and trying through your own sheer force of will to bring it into creation?

It's exhausting.

And . . . it doesn't work.

We can't step into God's calling over our life with a clenched fist of how we think the story should go. We can't wish away our monologue, longing for someone else's plotline. With a rewrite and a red-pen edit, clinging to this idea that we know better how the narrative should have unfolded. When we trust the Author, we trust the story.

Lately, I've been getting the same message over and over again. It's an image in my head that's as clear as any picture I've ever seen. It's of a balled-up fist, nails digging in. Broken. World-wearied. Exhausted from holding on far too tight for far too long. And the relief that comes when you Just. Let. Go.

Entitlement and attachment are trying to keep their grip on you. And there is only one way to break free.

Open your hand.

SLOW GROWTH PRAYER

GOD,

I'm sorry for every time I believed I could write the story better than you could. I'm sorry for how I get so set in my own plans and these ideas in my head of how things should go. I'm sorry for ever approaching you with entitlement and handing over my list of demands.

Lord, I know that when the Bible says you will give me the desires of my heart, that doesn't mean you are some genie granting every wish. It means that when I spend time with you, when I delight myself first in YOU, then you will place your promises in my heart of what will be, according to your plan.

I'm so tired from holding on so tight.

I am exhausted from trying to force everything.

Help me to let go and trust you, Lord.

Help me to finally find this place called surrender.

AMEN.

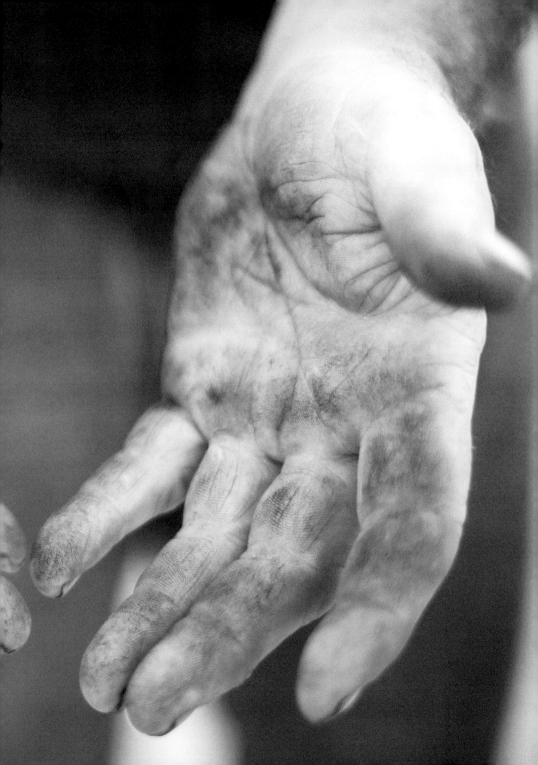

27

MOVE THE
DECIMAL POINT

*where once there was scarcity and not enough,
now abundance begins to take root*

Jesus then took the loaves, gave thanks, and distributed to those who were seated as much as they wanted. He did the same with the fish.

JOHN 6:11 NIV

JUSTIN AND I were sitting in our accountant Lisa's office. Our two chairs tucked side by side across the desk from hers, stacks of papers and blue folio-bound returns piled precariously between us, a plastic container of celebratory cupcakes from SUGAR being passed around.

Every year we bring an offering to Lisa in the form of our favorite cupcakes. It started out seven years ago when we begged her to take us on as last-minute clients—a "pretty please with SUGAR on top" if you will—when our previous accountant stopped returning emails a week before taxes were due and we found ourselves in a panic. She saved the day, and she's been doing our accounting ever since. And now every year, like a confectionary Ebenezer stone, we raise a tiny cake in remembrance of how God still sends supernatural help to his people when we need it most. Amen.

It was there, between bites of assorted lemon drop and German chocolate and "unicorn poop" tiny cakes, that I asked Lisa the question.

"So, how much money does someone have to make before taxes are never stressful again?"

Lisa didn't miss a beat. And I don't think I'll *ever* forget what she said to us next.

"The way people are with money when they are making $50,000 is the same way they are when they're making $500,000 or $5,000,000. If they were generous with one, they'll be generous with the other. If they were greedy or scarcity minded with one, that's the same way they'll be with more. If they were making mistakes with one, you can bet that's the same kinds of mistakes they'll make with the other. Except now the stakes are much higher. Those people aren't just making ten times the income, they're getting themselves into ten times the trouble."

She took her final bite. And I watched her shoulders shrug.

"Money is money. Just move the decimal point."

I don't know about you, but for a long time I was waiting until I got "there" (wherever there is) before I felt like I could really start to help people. I told myself a laundry list of lies about how until I had as many followers as *she* did, nobody was really going to care what I had to say. I believed that until my business was as big as *theirs* was, I had no business teaching others what I knew. I bought into this belief that until my bank account had what someone else's had in it, I wasn't in any position to give any away.

I kept waiting on God to multiply my circumstances before I believed he could ever use me.

When I hear that word *multiply*, it of course makes me think of Jesus feeding the five thousand. Jesus is up on a mountain with the disciples and they see a huge crowd coming toward them. And I love that the first thing Jesus does when he sees them, ever concerned with all the different ways that humans hunger, is ask, "Where can we buy bread to feed all these people?" (John 6:5 NLT). Even though we know he already knows the answer. The disciples tell him there isn't enough money to buy more bread. Philip says, "Even if we worked for months, we wouldn't have enough money to feed them!" (John 6:7 NLT). Everyone is wringing their hands, kicking the ground, staring down at their feet. Then one of them, Andrew, points to a boy who has five loaves of bread and two fish.

Can you imagine being the one in your Zoom work meeting to make *that* suggestion? "Hey guys, I know quarterly sales are off by 5,000 percent. But don't worry. Little Timmy here packed a lunch. We can just divide that up among all the shareholders!" In my head, this scene plays out with one of the other disciples looking directly into the camera and making a classic Jim Halpert face in response to such a Michael Scott suggestion. *"Thaaaat's not it."*

The Bible tells us there were five thousand men in the crowd, not counting women and children. So really it was probably closer to double or even triple that number. And here's Jesus with this little boy, five loaves of bread, and two fish.

Just a humble enough beginning for the miracle to really shine.

I've read the story of Jesus feeding the multitude I don't know how many times at this point. But it's a lot. And yet, until recently I somehow always missed something that was right there in black and white.

It's sort of like those memes that go around on the internet every now and then that ask you to close your eyes and picture: Does the Monopoly man wear a monocle? Did Curious George have a tail? Did Sinbad ever make a genie movie called *Shazaam*? (The answers are no, no, and no.) It's actually a whole phenomenon called the Mandela Effect, where people will *swear* they remember something happening one way, even though it did not.

For me, my Mandela Effect was that in my head all along Jesus clearly took the five loaves and two fish, put them in a nearby wicker basket, said a little blessing, and tapped the top like a magician putting on a show. And the five loaves were instantly transformed into five thousand. With a wave of his hand, Jesus moved the decimal point.

There is a little known, rather obscure 1980s movie starring Val Kilmer called *Real Genius* about a school for these incredibly gifted teenagers who, unbeknownst to them, are being used to develop a "laser weapon" for the CIA. (Side note: You have to love the commitment to accuracy the filmmakers had in using such technical terms.) But being the real geniuses that they are, the students figure it out just in time to save the day and—spoiler alert—end up redirecting the laser to instead heat up a house-sized aluminum ball of popcorn kernels in the bad guy professor's living room. Pretty soon the house is bursting at the seams with popcorn. It's pouring out every window, until it eventually knocks down the front door with its overwhelming abundance.

That's how I pictured the miracle of the loaves and fishes in my head: people would be absolutely *swimming* in bread. It would be rolling down the side of the mountain, this artisanal avalanche. Everyone would start building dough-men and making dough-angels. They would be absolutely knocked over with God's abundance. *Cloudy with a Chance of Garlic Knots.*

But then I go back and I read it again. And I see something I never saw before.

> When they had all had enough to eat, he said to his disciples, "Gather the pieces that are left over. Let nothing be wasted." So they gathered them and filled twelve baskets with the pieces of the *five barley loaves* left over by those who had eaten. (John 6:12–13 NIV, emphasis mine)

The *five* barley loaves.
I missed it. And there's a chance you have too.

Scripture doesn't tell us exactly how Jesus performed this miracle. Were the five loaves immediately multiplied into five thousand? Did a new piece of bread appear every time one was taken? Did he make the people feel supernaturally full with only a morsel? Was it a *Honey, I Blew Up the Kid* situation, where the loaves were suddenly two stories high? It's not clear.

But here is what we do know: Jesus saw what the rest of the world dismissed as too small of an offering. He blessed it, gave thanks for it, and used it to feed thousands. But most of all, it was important to him that *none* of it be wasted.

Here is the other thing we see: the little boy, whose name we're never told, started with five loaves. And for all we know, he was sent home with only five loaves when he was done. Or maybe, for all we know, the twelve disciples took all twelve baskets and the boy was sent home with none. We can't really be sure. But what we do know is this: his outward circumstances did not change before Jesus could use him.

See, all along I've been looking down at these meager offerings in my hands, believing that God had to multiply *me* first before I could help anyone else. But God can take these scraps we bring to the table—these not-nearly-enough and not-there-yet humble beginnings—and use them to feed others in ways we will never understand.

And here's the real catch that we have to learn to be okay with if we are going to hand over our gifts to follow Jesus: the world may never know our name.

Sometimes when God is using us to serve others, that *will* involve him also multiplying us. He will promote the platform. He will increase the bank account. He will open the doors all in the name of reaching more people and bringing glory to his name.

But sometimes he won't.

Sometimes he will look at our modest offering and say, "That is plenty. I can use you right here, right where you are."

Your five loaves will stay five loaves. For now, the world will not know your name. You'll just be someone who was in the right place at the right time with the right provisions.

And what he wants to know from you and from me is, *Will that be enough for you?*

"If you never get rich, if you never get famous, if you're never someone the world considers a person of influence, but I used you and the gifts in your hands to feed thousands, or even just one . . . will that be enough for you?"

We believe we have to be more of something before we'll ever matter. But God is more interested in what's in our hearts. Because who we are with five loaves is who we'll be with five thousand. He is not asking us to multiply our circumstances before we can be of use to him. He's only asking us to be willing to invest what we have.

Because in God's economy, the inputs do not match the outputs. He can take our not enough and turn it into more than enough. He'll start with what you have.

And then he'll move the decimal point.

GOD,

Thank you for the times you keep us small enough so that the real miracle can shine. If it was all about us being enough of something, about us being perfect, polished, or plenty, then you might not get the glory when the true provision comes through.

Thank you, Lord, that where you are involved, nothing is wasted.

For the one who is reading right now and feels like that little kid on the mountaintop—the one whose name nobody cares enough to know, the one whose gifts the world has dismissed as far too small—help them to remember that you often use the ones working behind the scenes to help change the world.

Help us to use every gift we have and offer it all up to follow you. Put us in the right place at the right time to use everything that's in our hands.

Thank you that you are still the God who is concerned with all the different ways that humans hunger.

And thank you for letting us be part of the miracle when you could so easily do it on your own.

AMEN.

SLOW GROWTH PRAYER

28

where once there was a prison of perfection, now empathy begins to take root

THE GIRL IN
THE OVERSIZED
SWEATSHIRT

Therefore, as God's chosen people, holy and dearly loved, clothe yourselves with compassion, kindness, humility, gentleness and patience.

COLOSSIANS 3:12 NIV

We go out in the world wearing the armor of the well-adjusted, the sword and shield of the over-achieved, the cape that covers all manner of our most secret identities. Brick by brick we build a facade that we think is everything the world wants to see.

But then, when we step back to admire our work, we realize we haven't built a monument to how far we've come but a wall that now stands between us and other people. These capes and masks we wear are not just barriers that keep everyone else out. They are also a prison of perfection that keeps us walled in.

*And we're suffocating.**

I USED TO WANT to buy a new outfit every time I went to a conference.

*Marantz, *Dirt*, 226.

It felt like a necessity. As crucial to my performance as some perfectly polished keynote slides and a well-rehearsed opening origin story. It was as though I didn't know how to walk out on that stage and actually feel like I belonged there if I hadn't just cut the tags off of something shiny and brand-new.

This uniform of mine, this superhero mask and cape—it had one fatal flaw. If you wore it more than once, it somehow seemed to lose all of its power. It would be sort of like walking into the Batcave one Dark and stormy (K)night only to realize the Caped Crusader had a whole closet full of Batsuits that were apparently as disposable as Bruce Wayne's income. It would be like finding out Batman was no longer bulletproof the second the clock struck midnight, when this outer covering of his lost all of its protective power.

Brand-new blazers and pearls became my Kevlar. The perfect tea-length dress, the one with just the right swoop in the skirt, was like a new form of body armor. No one could ever hurt me if I was wearing the right suit.

There is another picture of me when I was a kid. I'm a year older than in that photo with the crouched-down version of me. The same kinky-curly, untamed hair, though it's shorter. And apparently being held in place by one pair of oversized neon-orange sunglasses that I don't remember ever owning. I'm standing next to a four-lane highway with cars flying by—this wide-open road of possibilities—arms stretched out wide in celebration. Evidently I was very excited at the prospect of heralding our arrival to New Hampshire, the Granite State, as the welcome sign behind me makes clear. It was the farthest I had ever traveled out of West Virginia up until that point.

And it felt like a mile-marker moment in my life.

But what stands out to me most, what I remember more than anything, is that I'm wearing a sweatshirt that is at least three sizes too big for me. A fact made only more evident by these wide-open

outstretched arms. To this day I'm not sure if the sweatshirt was Grandma Goldie's and I was only wearing it because I was cold. Or if it was mine and we had gotten it at some yard sale. What I remember is how it makes me feel.

This girl in the oversized sunglasses and the oversized sweatshirt, practically swimming in all this *too much*.

To me it has always been the very picture of *not enough*.

And I suppose she was the girl I always imagined walking out on stage anytime I wasn't wearing something brand-new. She was the one who would be left standing up there exposed. Behind all these protective barriers, she was the alter ego I was trying so hard to keep safe.

FOR YEARS IN OUR BUSINESS, anytime Justin and I would speak at a conference, I believed I had to show up and play the part of successful speaker and business owner if I was going to be welcome on those stages. I believed I had to show up and be The Most Put-Together

Woman in the Room. I would wear the right outfits and casually drop the right numbers—the decimal point moving us into our six figures, the 10K in our starting packages. We used words like *boutique* and *high-end*. And we focused all our energy on being *very* big and impressive.

And it's not like any of it wasn't true. It was. We just weren't being honest with ourselves about what really mattered, what we really wanted our legacy to stand for. For years, we stood onstage and gave helpful business talks. And some people in the crowd would always stay afterward to say thank you and ask questions.

But the first time I ever stood onstage and showed a picture of the trailer I grew up in—and a picture of that kinky-curly-haired girl I had tried so long to hide—*that day* there was a line that ran all the way out the back of an at-capacity ballroom that seated one thousand. It spilled down the hallway and took over the entire main lobby. And after two hours of this, security finally had to come and break it up.

Here's the thing. All those people weren't there to talk to me because I was so put-together, polished, or impressive. And they weren't there because they liked my outfit either. Nothing about The Most Put-Together Woman in the Room is what drew them close to me.

They stood in that line, waited as long as it took, because they wanted to come up and tell me face-to-face, "I am the Girl in the Trailer too."

They said things to me like, "I would have never guessed from looking at you" and "You are the first person in this industry I have seen up on that stage who grew up like I did." For a lot of them, I was the very first person they had ever said those words to out loud as an adult, whispered this truth about how they had grown up. All this time they had been burying it there just below the surface, believing like I had that it disqualified them.

A few years later, when *Dirt* came out, people started sending me messages in my DMs with pictures of their own trailers that they grew

> ## OUR ORIGIN STORIES NEVER HAD TO BE PERFECTLY POLISHED OR WELL REHEARSED IN ORDER TO MATTER.

up in. I now have a whole folder on my phone filled with them. I can tell you right now, that folder means more to me than any spotlight moment I have ever had on a stage.

The irony—the very *futility*—of perfectionism is this: We believe we have to show up and be perfect in order to belong, in order to be accepted. When in reality, all we're doing is pushing people away.

Sometimes I think we get so busy putting on our masks and our capes that we forget to let people in. And sometimes I think we get so busy looking at other people's pretty lives that we forget to lean in and look a little closer for the story behind the facade, these suffocating walls that stand between us. But there's so much beauty in the brokenness if we'll only look for it. And there's so much honor in the miles we have already come.

It turns out our origin stories never had to be perfectly polished or well rehearsed in order to matter. We just had to be willing to go first. To let down these protective barriers. To show up with vulnerability. To lean in with empathy. And to connect with just one other human in kindness.

If I could go back and talk to that girl in the oversized sweatshirt, I would tell her not to worry too much about everything she thinks she is missing now. I would tell her that she will be kinder, gentler, and more empathetic for having gone through it.

And that someday *her* story is going to change way more lives than a woman in perfect pearls and a brand-new navy blazer ever could.

SLOW GROWTH PRAYER

GOD,

Thank you for how every day you are setting us free from this self-imposed prison of perfection.

Thank you for how you are reminding us to stop layering on the buttercream frosting and allow people to see the parts of us that are soft and delicate, in danger of crumbling. Because that vulnerability is where true connection is found, not in hiding behind these pretty, polished protective barriers we think will somehow make us more acceptable in the eyes of the world.

We know shiny is a stiff-arm, God. A Heisman pose. And we are so tired of holding people at arm's length simply because it feels safer than being seen up close.

Give us the courage to keep showing up just as we are.

Give us the courage to lean in.

We never know who it may make brave enough to come stand face-to-face with us, look us in the eye, and say . . . "me too."

AMEN.

29

where once there was frustration, now freedom begins to take root

IT GETS MESSY
IN THE MIDDLE

But do not forget this one thing,
dear friends: With the Lord a
day is like a thousand years, and a
thousand years are like a day. The
Lord is not slow in keeping his promise,
as some understand slowness. Instead
he is patient with you,
not wanting anyone
to perish, but
everyone to come
to repentance.

2 PETER 3:8–9 NIV

DO YOU WANT to know something?

Most days I feel like I'm walking uphill, waist-deep in quicksand, face-first against the resistance of a hurricane-force wind tunnel . . . while sipping on molasses. Because the forward progress is just that slow. That is what it's like when you feel stuck in the day-to-day.

The truth is, I'm big on the "Headlines God."

He was the one who took the little girl in the leaky trailer and set her down gently right in the middle of

Yale Law School as if she had somehow always belonged there. He was the one who took the twenty-four-year-old me, the one who swore she would *never* get married, and had her meet her husband of now almost fifteen years on a three-day free trial to Match.com. And he was the one who took this grown-up woman who still can't stand the smell of mildew and used it to open the door to her buying her dream home in the form of a little fixer-upper-in-foreclosure by the sea when a pipe burst on the third floor. It ran for three days, flooded the entire house, and then sat abandoned for six months.

Until the whole place reeked of mildew . . . and felt like home.

These are only some of the headlines of my life. If I were keeping a faith scrapbook, a covenant collage of answered prayers, these would be the clippings that would fill the pages. I would add in spreads about the little five-year-old girl who dreamed of one day being a writer, and then use a glue stick and glitter to layer on a photo of a forty-year-old me sitting with my laptop by a window overlooking the water. There would be sheets filled with gold stars and golden retrievers, an entire folio full of fun vacations and adventures, and full spreads ripped right out of the J.Crew catalog.

These are the places where I know God loves me. These mountain-top moments. These cinematic, happy-ending, heart-swelling scenes.

But what about when you wake up the next morning and the story goes on? When you roll out of bed, rub your eyes, and simply go on living because your heart is still beating, there is still breath in your lungs, and you are more than just the last good thing that happened to you. What about when the day-to-day turns into months and months? What about when it's been so long since your last happy headline that you aren't sure God is ever going to show up on the page again?

Where is God in the small print of our lives?

"NO SETBACK, NO STORY."

Have you ever watched a great underdog story, where the lead character tries out for the team or tries to get the job or goes in for that first dream audition . . . and they instantly get all the success they ever wanted?

End scene. Roll credits. Cue the inspirational score.

Yeah, me neither.

They don't make movies like that. And we don't watch them.

We want someone who had to fight their way to the goal. Someone who faced failure and disappointment and watched from the sidelines as someone else got everything they ever wanted. And they still somehow found it inside themselves to rise. To get back up, dust themselves off, and live to fight another day. We want our heroes to have faced and overcome hardship.

And we don't hold it against them when they stumble.

Rudy isn't Rudy if he gets picked first for the team. The Goonies aren't the Goonies if their motto is "Goonies get everything they ever wanted." And oh how we love to talk about how many times J. K. Rowling was rejected before everyone could see the magic in a character who always had the scars to prove it.

No one ever watches an underdog movie and thinks to themselves, "Oh, this loser again. Why don't they just quit already? Don't they realize by now that they don't have what it takes?"

We don't think that about the characters we root for. And yet we think that about ourselves every day. We feel like every failure is fatal and every disappointment is a sign that we aren't cut out for this. We see our struggles and we want to quit. But we forget the most important rule of the underdog movie.

If we skip the setbacks, we forfeit the story.

Let this be your reminder that small steps add up. Imperfect progress still moves you forward. Action breeds clarity, so do something.

You'll either get it right or you'll learn something. Either way, it's a win.

But let this also be your reminder that God rarely shows us the whole road map right from the beginning. And that's hard. It's frustrating. As a person who is often guilty of reading the last page of a book before I start it, I am someone who loves to know exactly how the story turns out. Like I said, I am a headlines kind of girl.

But that kind of thinking means living your entire life for only a few mountaintop moments and *missing* every other messy, beautiful day in between.

Getting to see the whole staircase before you take the first step? I'm here to tell you it doesn't work that way.

Way more often, it looks like climbing a staircase in a thick, dense fog. Only the steps are made of some sort of sticky marshmallow substance like that one scene in *A Nightmare on Elm Street*, which I am apparently still not over. So that every step you take feels like you're stuck, sinking, and going ten times slower than you should be. As the Freddy Krueger of Fear is right behind you, ripping at your heels with his knives-for-fingers and gaining on you fast.

Great. Who feels like living the *dream* now?

But there is freedom there if you look for it.

It's *supposed* to be messy in the middle. It's supposed to get sticky right when you're trying your hardest to move forward. It's supposed to be at times harder, more uncertain, and taking way longer than you ever could have imagined.

Other people don't have some magic bullet. They aren't sprinting up the same staircase in stilettos like some goal-crushing Elle Woods. "What? Like it's hard?"

They stumble. They fall. They're feeling their way through the fog the same way you are. You can stop assuming everyone else is more qualified, more equipped than you are.

Through all of this, I'm learning, there is beauty in the tension. In leaning in to listen for the wisdom in the pause. Bating your breath long enough for the *dot dot dot* to make sense. And waiting for the next right thing to reveal itself one materializing step at a time.

Something incredible happens over time, something that might be very hard to believe right now if you're finding yourself waist-deep in your own marathon of molasses. Inch by inch, day by day, this work you're doing . . . it adds up. It counts. It matters. It *changes* things. One painfully slow, unseen, uncelebrated, unsatisfying inch at a time.

So if you're feeling stuck. If you're feeling lost. If you feel like nothing is moving and no one in the world will notice if you go ahead and give up . . . I'm here to tell you, it just takes longer than you think. The headlines day will be here soon enough. And there will be so much to celebrate. But in the meantime, you are being refined in the fire of faithfully showing up.

Inch by inch you are becoming a person who stays the course.

Even when it gets messy in the middle.

GOD,

I thank you for all the ways you are teaching me to love and live for every day of my life—both the headline days and the small-print ones.

Thank you for who I am becoming and the work you are doing in me on those messy middle days.

Thank you, God, for making us into people who stay the course. We know that one day when we cross that finish line, we'll get to show other people that it can be done.

But in the meantime, we believe that even when we feel stuck, even when we feel like we're getting it all wrong, we are right where we are supposed to be.

We'll just keep taking the next step you show us in faith and obedience.

Believing that the path will be made clear as we go.

AMEN.

SLOW GROWTH PRAYER

No

30

BEGIN AGAIN

where once there was constant striving, now the courage to start over begins to take root

*Forget the former things; do
not dwell on the past. See, I am
doing a new thing! Now it springs
up; do you not perceive it? I am
making a way in the wilderness
and streams in the wasteland.*

ISAIAH 43:18–19 NIV

BEGIN AGAIN.

I'm not sure there is anything more blistering to slow growth than . . . *starting over.*

It is one thing to ask us to grow slow and steady over the long haul so that one day we may walk among the giants. It is quite another for our hopes and plans and good progress to be clear-cut down in one fell swoop and reduced in an instant to a blank slate of scarred, scorched earth. The tattered blueprint confetti of our best-laid plans placed gingerly in our shaking hands as we watch the pieces take lift and slowly float away on currents of hot air, like dandelion dander drifting in the late August wind.

There is no perfectly scaled set of drawings for finding yourself back at square one.

And those moments can give rise to the greatest doubt each one of us may ever face: *Perhaps there was never a plan for me at all.*

In those moments when you've gone big, swung for the fences, felt the fear, and pressed forward anyway—those times when you've done exactly what you're supposed to do when it comes to boldly chasing a dream and you've come up short anyway—it can be hard not to feel like maybe God has forgotten about you.

That maybe you are just a somebody who was always meant to be a little bit of a *nobody.*

On some level all of us are walking around with this one fear repeating in our minds like a steady drumbeat as soft and familiar as our own heartbeat. So imperceptible at times that we can almost forget it's even there. All the while thudding out what could possibly be the greatest disappointment of our days this side of heaven.

"I am just afraid that my life will pass unnoticed."

For many of us, we have spent the first decades of our adult lives grinding out a good life. We traded our messy narrative for a pretty two-story house. We swapped our most hidden secret scars for a well-emblazoned handbag we want the world to see. We walked through the fire and came out the other side with our gold bands and golden retrievers.

And we took this grit of ours and turned it into our favorite pair of pretty pearl earrings.

We have spent years of our lives acquiring the right house, the right car, the right clothes, the right job, the right marriage, the right kids. All of this *right* we've done with our lives, only to watch it crumble

"TIME HAS A WAY OF *unraveling* EVEN THE MOST *tightly* STITCHED DREAMS."

when something unexpected goes so very *wrong*. An illness. A divorce. A financial disaster. A devastating loss. An unprecedented pandemic.

I have friends I have walked through life with for the last twenty years, ever since those first few days of freshman orientation at West Virginia University. We all started out as these bright-eyed and ambitious forces to be reckoned with, determined to go out and make a better life for our future daughters than we ever had. We all had stories we were running from, and we felt like we could run faster if we stood shoulder to shoulder and side by side. We were ready to set the world on fire.

But time has a way of unraveling even the most tightly stitched dreams.

One by one, I have watched these friends walk through the flames. Through marriages ending. Through illnesses of parents. Through job losses. And through dream houses built right side up but eventually sold upside down in the ultimate display of bubbles bursting.

I've watched women like me who were running so hard from failure that they stumbled their way into what the world deemed success. And then I watched them lose it all and face the pale-blue dawning of a new day back at zero, a new day starting over.

What do you do when you've spent twenty years of your life acquiring what the world says matters, only in the process to lose the thing you can never get back: time.

If tomorrow it was all gone, what would you do differently?

Really sit with that question for a while.

If you had the chance to start over, to blank-slate it, to do it all over again today . . . what would remain? What would you go through the hard work of rolling up your sleeves to build again? And what doesn't really seem to matter to you that much anymore?

When I ask myself these questions, I realize I have spent way too much in my life—both time and money—trying to be enough of something for people who were never really *for* me. People who did not want to see me win, who did not wish good things for my life. These were not the people who were clapping when my name was finally called.

And yet they were the first people I would think of when I thought about all the ways I could be *more.*

I posed a question to Kim recently in one of our monthly video calls because she is someone who has walked with me from the height of achieving for my worth to now being a person who has started to know this taste of freedom.

I said, "When you think about me in those earliest days, what was the greatest symptom of this achieving disease?"

She only had to think about this for a second.

"I'd say it was two things." In the weight of her pause, I began to trace and retrace the handle of my favorite coffee cup. Waiting for the double hammer of her words to drop.

"One . . ." Kim always begins by numbering things, drawing out the count a beat longer than you'd expect, savoring it in her homegrown Georgia drawl. "You only saw success as this upward, linear mobility. It was this ladder you were climbing, where you always had your eyes on jumping to the next rung. You were very focused on what other people were doing and what that meant about you—how much faster or slower they were climbing compared to you. And for you, any movement backward at all, or even sideways for that matter, or, God forbid, stuck standing still . . . you saw that as *failure.*"

IF TOMORROW IT WAS ALL GONE, WHAT WOULD YOU DO DIFFERENTLY?

I nod my head silently at this through the screen. Every word she's spoken is true, and there's no point in trying to qualify it with empty explanations or interruptions.

"B . . ." Kim also has this tendency of jumping back and forth between letters and numbers in her counting, which I always smile at but never bring up because I don't want to break her flow.

I was tapping my thumb now against the ceramic of the mug, sending little shock waves through the lukewarm coffee inside. My eyes averted down, avoiding hers, waiting for the words I already knew were coming.

"B, your priorities were always way off. You weren't taking care of yourself. You weren't taking time to fill up. And all the things and people that matter most to you, they were only ever getting the crumbs of what you had left over." Once again, these crumbs of my life spilled out between us.

This one hurts more to hear. But only because it's heartbreaking.

It's heartbreaking to think about the people you will one day give anything to have just a few more minutes with being the very same ones who spent years only getting the least of you, your leftover scraps.

Annie Dillard said, "How we spend our days is, of course, how we spend our lives."* We spend our lives terrified of this thought: "I am just afraid that my life will pass unnoticed." When really we should be terrified that *we* are the ones who are missing it. We are the ones who have forgotten how to see what really matters.

If you have found yourself at a place in life where you have spent everything trying to keep up, trying to get to the top of the ladder only to find out all along it was leaned against the wrong building, have the courage to start over. Have the courage to rebuild better.

Have the courage to *begin again*. ▪

*Annie Dillard, *The Writing Life* (New York: HarperCollins, 1989), 31.

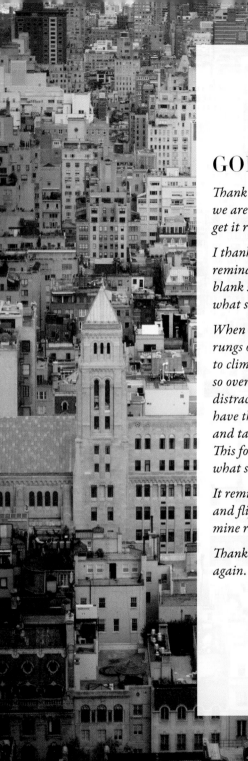

GOD,

Thank you that by your grace, every day we are breathing is another day to try to get it right.

I thank you for the hard times that remind us what really matters. Those blank slates that allow us to decide what stays.

When I've put all my priorities on the rungs of the wrong ladder I keep trying to climb. When my life has become so overstuffed with the "good" that it distracts me from the great. You, Lord, have this way of coming into my life and taking everything out of the room. This forces me to decide only by addition what stays.

It reminds me to put first things first and flips these upside down priorities of mine right side up again.

Thank you for the chance to begin again.

AMEN.

standing

TA

walk among the giants

31

God's asking us to shine our light in a dark world

SPARKS LIGHTING UP
THE WAY HOME

*You are the light
of the world. A city
set on a hill cannot be
hidden. Nor do people light
a lamp and put it under a
basket, but on a stand, and it
gives light to all in the house.*

MATTHEW 5:14–15

I ONCE HAD THE AUTHOR Ian Morgan Cron on my podcast.

He was there to talk about his book *The Road Back to You*, the Enneagram, and how whatever type we get is not really our true selves. It simply represents the mask that we learned to put on at some point when we were little. Because we believed this was the version of us we had to become in order to be loved.

For a long time I thought I was an Enneagram Three (Achiever) with a strong Four wing (Individualist). Now I believe it's possible it might be the other way around. Either way, I can tell you this: the mask I wear is suffocating.

It tells me that I don't just have to achieve big goals in order to win someone's approval. It says I have to achieve something *so big* that *no one* has ever hit goals quite like that before . . . if I am ever going to be loved. If my story is ever going to matter.

As I was telling Ian this, we got to talking about how we sometimes have to journey out into the world in order to finally understand the things we experienced when we were growing up. I told him how, as I have gotten older, there has been a *softening* in me that can only come with time. An understanding that comes only with age. I read him these words from *Dirt*:

> You get older and you realize just how hard being an adult really is. . . . You get older and you mess up. A lot. . . . And empathy floods like warm, golden light where once the stark winter landscape of bitterness used to reside. Like sparks of understanding lighting up the night sky.*

Right there—in the middle of a breath, in the middle of a pause—Ian hit me with something that knocked the wind right out of me: "I think we spend the whole first half of our life like the parable of the talents, trying to go out in the world and make an income with our gifts. But the second half is like the parable of the prodigal son. . . . *We're all just trying to find our way back home*."†

I burst into tears right there in the middle of the recording.

Not the sweet, endearing, single tear rolling down your cheek, voice ever-so-slightly choked up but then you quickly recover kind of crying. No, it was the "hold on, we have to stop recording while I grab a paper towel from across the room and blow my nose" kind of falling to pieces. And it was not pretty. Or *professional*.

---

*Marantz, *Dirt*, 248.
†Ian Morgan Cron, *The Mary Marantz Show* (podcast), episode 52, June 23, 2020.

Up until that point, I had never cried on my own show. Sure, I had interviewed plenty of other people who had gotten choked up while telling their stories. And plenty of times I had even teared up at what they were saying. But this was different. This wasn't an empathy cry at someone else's pain.

This was like a pinprick to a water balloon.

An overinflated, oversaturated, long overdue bursting of the dam.

Have you ever been outside on one of those days when a storm is brewing? When the raw nerve endings of thunderclouds feel electric on your skin and the hair on the back of your neck starts to stand on end? When the air feels so heavy and thick, so pregnant with possibility, that it feels like if you reached out and tapped it, it would give way in a downpour?

This was like someone had reached through the line and tapped the rawest nerve endings of the hole in my heart. And the dam had just given way in a downpour.

I knew exactly what Ian meant.

In the parable of the talents found in Matthew 25:14–30, Jesus tells the story of a master who, before setting off on a long journey, entrusts his three servants with different sums of his wealth. To one he gives five talents, to another he gives two talents, and to the last he gives only one talent. When the man returns, he finds that the first servant has taken the five talents and doubled the amount to ten talents. The one who had been entrusted with two talents has doubled them to four. But the servant who was only given one talent had been so afraid of what would happen if he failed that he hid his talent. Buried it in the darkness away from the world where he believed it would be safe.

Some people will read that story and know that they are like the third servant, hiding their talents away from a waiting, watching world. They would rather bury their gifts and what they are capable

"WE'RE ALL
JUST TRYING
TO *find*
OUR WAY
BACK *home*."

—Ian Morgan Cron

of than risk failing and losing it all. Rather than risk disappointing someone. Once again, suddenly it feels safer to create nothing than to create failure.

I get that. I have been that person.

But I have also been an extreme version of the other two. I read a story like that and all I can hear is how you have to double down—go out into the world and make *more* of yourself—if you want to please the people around you. If you are ever going to win their love.

I have spent years trying to take what I've been given and somehow become more, believing that this story of mine would only ever matter, would only ever be a story worth telling, if I went out into the world and ended up with more to show for it than what I started with. A *lot* more. Why simply double what you started with when you could increase it tenfold? Why multiply it by ten when you could move the decimal point even further?

The problem with me and the parable of the talents is that all I've ever seen is the *more*.

But if we look closer, we see something else there waiting for us. We notice that the one with five came back with only ten. And the one with two came back with only four. And yet each was called a good and faithful servant. Wherever they were just one—for every *one* talent they had—they went out and created just one more. This could be a coincidence, just random numbers chosen for the story. But I also believe that Jesus was always intentional with the stories he told and the lessons they were meant to teach us.

Maybe rather than teaching us about more, Jesus is telling us what is *enough*.

He is not asking us to go out and move the decimal point. We already know that is his job. He is just asking that we not hide these gifts and abilities away. He's asking that we not bury them in a scarcity mindset, more afraid of failing than thinking about the good it could do. He's asking that we not let fear have the final word.

More than anything, he's asking us to go out and shine our light in a dark world. Even if it's only for *one* other person. Because our truest gifts are the ones that, although we might one day get to do for the many, we would still be willing to do for only the one. If just one other person is helped by what we share with the world, that would be enough for us.

Wherever we are just one, we are called to go out and create just one more. To pay it forward in love. A candle losing nothing by lighting another candle.

Until like sparks lighting up a night sky . . . it's easier for *all* of us to find our way home.

GOD,

I want to thank for you the softening, the empathy, the wisdom that comes with time.

Thank you for these gifts we've been given, and thank you for the chance you give us to help light up a dark world.

I praise you that every day you are pointing the way back home, to a place where warm, golden light floods and we are no longer searching for something in the dark, something this world can never provide.

Thank you that it was never about us becoming so much more of something before we could be loved. It was always just about inviting us to be part of something bigger than ourselves.

Sometimes we have to go out into the world to find our way back to you, God.

Thank you for the lights that are guiding us home.

AMEN.

Nº

32

but we are not called to be like the world

THE WORLD
REWARDS ACHIEVING

Do not love the world or
the things in the world.
If anyone loves the world,
the love of the Father is not
in him. For all that is in the
world — the desires of the flesh
and the desires of the eyes and
pride in possessions — is not from
the Father but is from the world.
And the world is passing away
along with its desires, but whoever
does the will of God abides forever.

1 JOHN 2:15–17

DON'T LET ANYONE convince you that you can't live a big life.

Don't let anyone convince you that you can't live a small, simple, but profoundly impactful life either.

Big or small, the magic happens when we chase the life that *we* are being called to and have been created for. It is the place where our gifts can best help and serve and impact other people. Whether that's making dinner and reading stories for the family right in front of you or running a business in your own community or writing words for people you might never get the chance to hug in person.

I want to be real here. If it feels like the world rewards achieving, and thereby overachievers, that's because it does. It *absolutely* does.

The world wants to hear from the ones with the blue check marks. The followers. The big bank accounts. The successful businesses. The perfect homes. The curated wardrobes. The luxury vacations. And in all this noise, it's no wonder we are absolutely *choking* in the weeds.

The world rewards *fast*. It is a big fan of the overnight success and it is not in the business of singing the praises of the long, slow climb. It is not interested in the process or the journey. It will seldom take notice of the ones who need a little more time.

But you know what? I do. I notice them. I see greatness in those who choose to dig a little deeper. Those who are not satisfied unless they build with integrity. Those who believe with their whole heart that a job worth doing isn't worth a thing unless it is also worth doing well. Those who choose to pursue excellence as if working for the Lord. To those who seek respect, not attention, and those more interested in growing deep, not just high, I just want to say that *I see you*.

I see you and the world needs more of you. Keep digging. Keep showing up. Good things take time. *Real* things take time. And just know that there are some of us out here who think that how long you've been at this is one of the most interesting parts of your story.

This is your reminder that the world will try again and again to tell you what success looks like. It is an expert in using phrases like "supposed to" and "what everyone else is doing." But in my experience, supposed to and what everyone else is doing will almost always lead you down the wrong path.

Certainly down the most crowded one.

There is a reason the Bible reminds us, "Do not love the world or the things in the world. If anyone loves the world, the love of the Father is not in him. For all that is in the world—the desires of the flesh and the desires of the eyes and pride in possessions—is not from the Father but is from the world. And the world is passing away along with its desires, but whoever does the will of God abides forever" (1 John 2:15–17).

What I'm saying is, the world gets it wrong a lot.

Lately, I've been thinking so much about this one idea that keeps coming back to me. It whispers to me. It keeps calling me back home.

I want to live a life that feels better on the inside than it looks on the outside.

I have spent most of my adult life trying to build these glass-castle empires—shiny on the outside, a six-by-eight containment cell—just to keep the world from throwing stones. Just so I could show how far I'd come. Just so one other person would be proud of me.

But I never once stopped to ask if the life I was building was one that I was actually proud of *myself*.

I am so thankful for how this slow growth is forging character in us long before the eyes of the world are upon us. What a gift it is that before there ever is attention on us, there will be integrity. One thing I used to remind our photography students of over and over was, "Don't ask for rain and then not pack an umbrella." This work that is being done in us now is preparing us to be set apart. Big or small, the

> *I WANT TO LIVE A LIFE THAT FEELS BETTER ON THE INSIDE THAN IT LOOKS ON THE OUTSIDE.*

places we are being called will be far more impactful . . . *because* we didn't get there overnight.

Today, more than anything, I want you to remember this.

You have the right to remake your life from the inside out. You have the right to say, "Enough achieving, enough performing, enough striving . . . I choose rest." You were not put here to chase the checklist of someone else's dreams. And neither was I. We are not bound to their hustle or their busy or their grind or their priorities. This is our chance to redefine what *we* think it is to win.

We are not called to spin our wheels without intention, hoping to gain some ground by the sheer perpetual motion of it all. Hoping that if we just start moving, just show up looking put-together and important enough, then failure won't find us.

We are called to walk this dirt road home with wide-open eyes on the path that is set before us. We are called to focus and rest and deep work and doing that thing we have been most gifted to do.

Remember this.

You don't have to hustle more, weigh less, earn more, sleep less, spend more, slow down less, people-please more, or say no less in order for you or your story to matter.

You already do. It already does.

GOD,

Thank you for all the ways you are setting us apart. Thank you for showing us again and again that what this world offers is the kind of emptiness that will only ever numb but never satisfy.

I praise you, God, for all the ways you are more interested in our character than our popularity count. Our impact more than whether we were impressive.

Big or small, Lord, help us to live these lives that are profoundly impactful. The ones that feel better on the inside for the purpose we are pursuing than how they could ever look on the outside to a world that keeps getting it so wrong.

This world is passing away along with all its desires, God.

But we have our eyes on abiding in you forever.

AMEN.

N<u>o</u>

33

THE HABIT
OF CELEBRATING

if we're not careful, we could spend our whole lives climbing

This is the day that the LORD has made; let us rejoice and be glad in it.

PSALM 118:24

JUSTIN AND I have gotten in the habit of keeping mini bottles of champagne in our refrigerator.

We do those little LaMarca splits—minis, piccolos, "personal poppers" if you prefer—perfect for toasting at a moment's notice. And at only one glass each, it's all of the bubbles without any of the regret.

And yes, before you think it, I *know* it's not technically champagne but prosecco, being that these little bottles aren't from a particular region in France but Italy. But hey, cut me some slack. It took me *years* to learn how to say Veuve Clicquot. And I think I still have a complex about it.

Plus, it's not really the point.

The point is, we have gotten in the *habit* of celebrating.

As someone who spent years achieving for her worth, somewhere along the line I lost the art of celebration. It got to the point where I would check that one box, cross that goal off my list, get the happy email I *dreamed* of reading for years . . . and one second later, *immediately* be on to the next thing. Full steam ahead.

It's like I didn't know how to get out of my own head to actually be present in that moment. I somehow couldn't come down from my neural synapses throwing sparks like a downed power line long enough to land in my own, actual, real life. To see and feel and hear and touch and taste what it really felt like in that moment when a prayed-for dream came true. I was only glancing at a blurry version of it in my periphery, my eyes laser-focused straight ahead on what was next. I could barely hear the muffled voices of friends who were happy and cheering for us, because they were quickly drowned out by the shouts of what the world said I was still missing.

And all I knew in that moment when I got there was that it didn't *feel* like what I thought it would feel like.

Some of us don't celebrate because we think it still isn't big enough compared to what someone else is doing. We don't think the world will see it as worthy.

Some of us don't celebrate because it will only point out how far behind we really are, how far we still have to go. We feel silly celebrating something we "should" have already achieved, so we think it's not worth pointing out. It's not yet worth being proud of.

And some of us don't celebrate because we feel like if we let up for even a moment—if we so much as blink—we will lose our edge, lose our momentum, the boulder will roll back down the mountain, and we will fall even further behind.

But for almost *all* of us, it really boils down to what someone else already has.

We look around and we tell ourselves this lie: until I'm where *they* are, I can't celebrate these wins. Except that one-liner rule becomes a lifelong sentence. When we finally do get to that mountaintop they were standing on and turn around to take in the view—to finally get to see what *they* saw—we realize they are now already three more mountains ahead.

So we spend our whole lives *climbing*.

We spend our days never really satisfied with where we are, never really present and accounted for in our own lives, never getting around to celebrating these wins along the way because we are always focused on the next goal up ahead. We have lost the art of letting life happen and unfold exactly how it was meant for us. We have lost the art of letting life surprise us. We walk into all of our moments with a white-knuckle grip on how they should go.

And in the process, we have forgotten what it looks like to live life with an open hand.

A few months back, I was telling Coach Kim that when the day comes when I do hit all of these goals I have for myself as an author, I already know that it won't feel like what I want it to feel like. I'll be too busy posting it on social media. I'll be too tired from months of launching. I'll wonder why some other book ranked higher.

It made me feel sick to my stomach to say those words out loud.

Kim chewed on this for a minute. I think it was just a little heart-breaking for her to hear too.

"Well." She clapped her hands together to make sure she had my attention. "What do you need to change about your life *right now*—your priorities, your perspective—so that when that day does come . . . you *don't* miss it?"

And so we buy the little bottles of champagne.

Like building up good muscle memory, we are getting in the *habit* now of celebrating along the way. Being present in our own actual, real lives. And honoring that slow growth is still progress.

Comparison robs you of the permission to enjoy your own life. You never once get around to celebrating any wins, big or small, because someone will have *always* just won bigger. There's a chance we could *always* look small in someone else's eyes. And that's the biggest theft of all right there.

That's the thing that should keep all of us up at night.

Because if we're not careful . . . we could spend our whole lives that way.

GOD,

This is the day that you have made. Teach me to rejoice and be glad in it.

This day in my life does not surprise you, Lord. You made it exactly for me.

Exactly in your timing.

Always on time and never late.

Help me to find my way back to celebrating, God. Celebrating every breath in my lungs, every beat of my heart for the magic they really are. This miracle where the rest of the world sees only mundane.

Help me to be present in my real, actual life, Lord. Slow me down so I really see it.

Every day that you open my eyes, every new day dawning, is a day that is worthy of all the confetti. Worthy of all the celebration.

And I will rejoice in it because of you.

AMEN.

SLOW GROWTH PRAYER

No

34

this is the crosshair intersection that has

the power to change lives

THE PLACE
WHERE OUR GIFTS
MEET OUR STORY

Having gifts that differ according to the grace given to us, let us use them: if prophecy, in proportion to our faith; if service, in our serving; the one who teaches, in his teaching.

ROMANS 12:6–7

THE PLACE WHERE our gifts meet our story has the power to change lives.

Or rather, *God* has the power to change lives. And in his goodness, he decides to include us in this important work. To come down and meet us right where we are and co-*create* with us because he loves seeing us use what he's given.

The Creator of the universe delights in involving *us* in his creation.

Let us never get in such a hurry that we miss the miracle in those words.

I had an epiphany when I was writing the proposal for *Dirt*, the pitch that we would eventually send out to publishers, where I included that line "the place where our gifts meet our story has the power to change lives." Really, I suppose the epiphany was twofold: one about our gifts and one about our story.

The first part of the epiphany I had was this: when we honor our gifts, we honor the Giver.

The truth is, I have always had a certain ability with words from the time I was little. It was something that teachers called out in me starting as early as kindergarten. And by the time I was in college, I even had an English 101 professor try to convince me to switch majors from political science and philosophy, just so I could join her department.

The irony here is that when I was little, all I ever dreamed of was singing from a stage. I would dance through the trailer, hairbrush in hand, singing my heart out to the latest country song. But, as it turns out, I'm somewhere just above Cameron Diaz in *My Best Friend's Wedding* when it comes to carrying a tune.

I prayed I would be given the gift of song. But instead, God gave me words.

For a long time, I dismissed that gift. There was a whole laundry list of gifts I would have much rather had. Singing. The ability to be popular and outgoing. Any recognizable ounce of athletic prowess.

We do that, don't we? That thing that comes naturally to us, we assume it's no big deal and must come easy to everyone else too. So we look down on our gifts, always wishing for what someone else has.

For a long time, anytime someone would use that word *storyteller* about me, it felt like a backhanded compliment. Like what they were really saying was that I needed to get to the point. Or that I was all story, no substance. But then I started to think about Jesus. Of all the ways he had available to him to teach—bullet points, how-to guides, complex algebraic algorithms and formulas accessible only to hidden figures and beautiful minds—of all those possible ways, Jesus chose story.

In teaching all of the most important lessons he had for humanity in his short time on earth, Jesus chose a method that was the most accessible to the most people. They did not have to be wealthy enough to gain access to books or educated enough to be able to read them. They just had to be able to listen. And learn.

It reminds me of the earliest days of Appalachia and this great tradition of storytelling that was born there out of necessity. When there weren't enough books—when there weren't enough people who could even read books if there were any—entire histories were passed down from generation to generation through the spoken word. It's why I come from a long line of great storytellers. And none more prolific than one J.R. Bess.

My dad knew the value of a good story. And he knew the value of hard work. Both of which he passed on to me.

This *Logger* to *Legacy*, if you will, wrapped up in the pages of a gilded, bound book called *Dirt*.

I heard once that human beings are actually hardwired down to our very neural pathways to learn and remember best through the method of story. That's why Jesus chose it. And when one story didn't make sense to the crowds, when the message wasn't quite getting through, what did he do? Did he then resort to bullet points and formulas for how to live this life? No.

He just told a better story.

I've spent a lot of time thinking about that since writing *Dirt*. In a lot of ways, I feel like I can't take any more credit for the words on those pages than I can for the color of my eyes. They are both something God gave me. When we honor the gift, we honor the Giver.

That's when the second part of the epiphany hit me hard.

The same can be said of my story.

I had no more control over being born when and where I was—growing up in that single-wide trailer as the daughter of a logger—than I had over the color of my eyes or the fact that I can write all day but could never carry a tune in a bucket. And here's the thing: *Dirt* doesn't happen without both of those things—words *and* story.

The place where your gifts meet your story has the power to change lives.

Ever since having that double epiphany in my own life, I haven't been able to unsee it in everyone around me. I see it in that coaching client who became an expert in systems and time management because her parents were always working late when she was little, so now she fiercely believes *moments matter.* I see it in my own Coach Kim, who has an incredible gift for pointing people to realize their potential for greatness, which she first discovered when she coached her crew team in college. She is now teaching other women how to stand firm in their place on the shore by first standing firm in hers.

God is using each of these women to change lives, to co-create with him, because they are standing in the crosshair intersection where their gifts meet their story.

He's asking you to do the very same thing today.

THERE'S A REALLY GOOD CHANCE that the biggest lie you are telling yourself right now is this right here: *There is no room for me.*

That idea you have? It's already been done.

That book you have in you? It's already been written.

That stage you want to speak on? It's already too overcrowded.

I get it. I really do. I mean, I wrote a book about going from humble beginnings to the Ivy League. Which is literally a book that has been written at least ten different ways.

But here's the thing. I can't change my story. I can't change the gifts God gave me. And I can't change the fact that I felt like he was asking me to use both.

I could only ask myself, What does it look like for *me* to tell the truth here?

Hemingway said, "All you have to do is write one true sentence. Write the truest sentence that you know."* C. S. Lewis said, "No man who bothers about originality will ever be original: whereas if you simply try to tell the truth (without caring twopence how often it has been told before) you will, nine times out of ten, become original without ever having noticed it."†

Let today be the day you start telling the truth. Let today be the day you start telling your story. Let today be the day you do something about that thing you can't go a day without thinking about.

God is asking you to stop dismissing these gifts he's given you while wishing for someone else's. To stop hiding your story away believing it disqualifies you from what he has for you. He wants you to lean into the places he's calling you. And to stand in unqualified awe at the miracle it is that we get to do this with him every single day for the rest of our lives if we choose to.

Let this be the year you commit to showing up. Show up and keep showing up. Tell the truth. As best you know how. You never know, it may be *your* voice that finally gets through to somebody.

Your story is not a mistake.

And the place where your gifts meet your story has the power to change lives.

Most of all, *yours.*

---

*Ernest Hemingway, *A Moveable Feast* (New York: Scribner, 1964), 11.
†C. S. Lewis, *Mere Christianity* (New York: Macmillan, 1943), 175.

SLOW GROWTH PRAYER

GOD,

We just want to stand before you today in unqualified awe that you would even think of including us this way.

The fact that we get to roll up our sleeves, get our hands muddy right beside you in the dirt of your creation, be so close to you that we can feel the vapor of your breath as you are exhaling life into the very dust we are finally shaking off . . . it is nothing short of a miracle.

Lord, you have never made another one of us.

Every work you create is an original.

Which means that when we are standing in the spot where our gifts meet our story, every single one of us has the ability to be a reflection of your love in this world that has never quite been seen before.

I just want to sit in that for a minute, God.

I don't want to be moving so fast that I miss it.

I have spent far too long missing it.

In this moment, I exhale right alongside you, Lord.

And all of creation is calling me home.

AMEN.

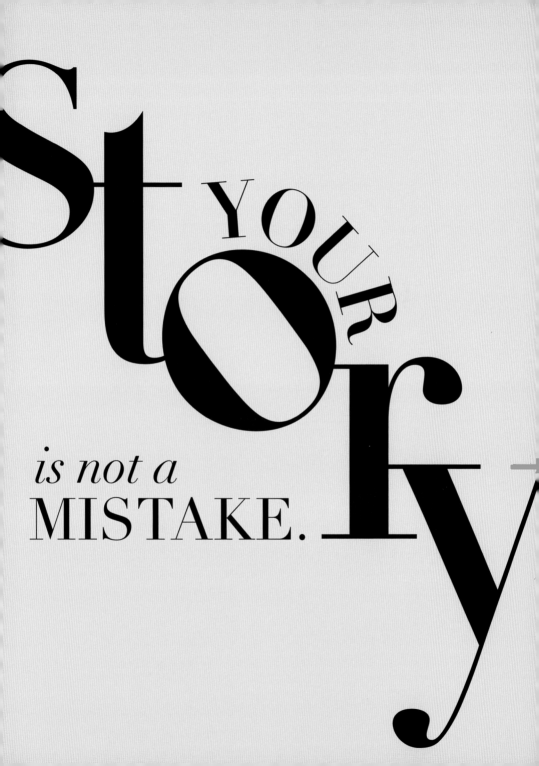

at a certain point, we all have to decide: are you all in?

No

35

A LOVE LETTER TO THE (AT LAST) EXHAUSTED

*Do not despise these small
beginnings, for the L*ORD
rejoices to see the work begin.

ZECHARIAH 4:10 NLT

ARE YOU ALL IN?

At a certain point we all have to decide the answer
to this question.

We are standing now just on the other side of our
Sharpie-mark-through-the-calendar moment. We gaze
out at the precipice of our After. The horizon of the
rest of our lives is unfolding before us, two roads now
diverging out in front. This inciting incident—we are
at last exhausted—has led us to this very moment. And
now, on this side of a journey that will hopefully leave
us utterly and forever changed by the end . . . we realize
how far we still have to go.

But do not despise these small beginnings.

The Lord of the universe rejoices just to see the work
begin.

I imagine myself once again sitting crisscross on the
floor across from God. Close enough for our knees
to touch. Close enough for him to play the hand slap

game if he wanted to. Ten different universes spinning at the ends of his fingertips, every axis trembling at his touch. Every supernova worshiping at his name.

But he still counts every hair on my head.

As we sit there together, he whispers, "Never wish away your story. One day these wounds are going to help so many people heal."

And at once my story is outside of my body, outside of every bitter stronghold that once held it. And it's orbiting there like a prism in the Father's hands. My entire life I have been looking at only one side, one facade, of what this story means. The truth as I remembered it. The mirror shattered into a million pieces. But now, there in his hands, I see all the different sides I never saw before. How they all fit together to form something more beautiful than I ever knew.

And finally I see all the places where the light gets in.

In that moment I decide: *this* is the story I'll tell.

My life will become one big worship song. Every part of this story, every one of these gifts. No longer will I be content with going out into the world and making them all about me. About the beautiful life I can build.

Now I stretch my arms out wide, at last on solid ground. I will go beyond just growing for myself. I will dig in before I ever try to grow up. I will operate out of the abundance, this fruit that can be shared and given away. This shade and shelter that can be provided to others.

Because that is how we get to walk among the giants.

We are staring in the face of our *after*. These two roads divide out in front of us now: a life lived only for ourselves or a life spent pouring it all out for God. Every talent, every profit, every part of the story—every good gift he's given us turned around and given right back to him.

And here in the silence, only one question remains.

Are you ALL in?

A LOVE LETTER to the exhausted, the beaten down, the spread-too-thin, the ones who feel like giving up. This one is for you.

That light in you hasn't gone out, my friend. You only think it has.

You only sit there in the darkness, surrounded by the smoke of a thousand smoldering embers snuffed out before their time, because you think that's all you have left in you. You only throw up your hands in defeat, refusing to search for a single spark in the shadows that surround you, because the tank already feels beyond empty anyway. You're running on the proverbial *E* . . . for exhausted. And what you know more than anything is that there is no flame without the fuel.

You've grown familiar with the coldness where once you knew what it was to feel the heat on your face. To feel the fire in your eyes. Let's be honest, friend: you once knew what it was to shine. To leap in great leaps. To stride in great strides. And to tightrope walk the outer precipice of your dreams without any fear of falling. You once knew what it was to fly. And now here you sit, thinking that you're grounded. That you'll never know what it is to catch air beneath you again. But the truth is—the real get-down-to-the-heart-of-it, nitty-gritty truth is—you've just forgotten that these roots give you the power to once again RISE.

You've tied up knot after knot in your heart, tethering up your actions in the tangled web of someone else's dreams. Of what they say success is. Of what the world tells us we should want when it (and okay, Bono) reminds us that we still haven't found what we're looking for. It tells us what we're not enough of. And it tells us what we're not at all. What we will never be. And it reminds us that everyone else around us is blessed with a muchness—a look at me, I have it all togetherness—that our broken hearts will never come to know.

And so one by one, the firefly sparks we used to throw off into this world blink and burn out until we're not sure where all the fireflies have gone. That fire in our eyes—the one that used to tell us who we

The truth is, the world needs more

LIGHTS

just like you.

are and what we stand for—is no longer staring back when we look in the mirror. Until we can hardly recognize this scattered ashes-to-ashes person who has taken our place.

I know you feel like that light in you has gone out. But trust me, because I've been there before too. You only think it has.

You have no idea what a lamplight you are in this world. You couldn't possibly know. Of the numbered masses who take shelter and warm themselves by the comforting constant of your fire. Of the lonely paths that you alone have been a lamp and a lantern for. Of the ways home you are lighting at this very moment. There are untold many whose lives have been made better, bigger, brighter because they happened to stumble upon you, and like a beacon in the darkness you helped them find their way again.

So I know it feels like that light has gone out for good. I know it feels like that fire you only sort of remember now must have actually belonged to someone else all along. But the truth is, this world needs you on fire burning up the darkness. For there is far too much darkness in the world. It needs you blazing the trail and lighting the way for those who come behind you. You have no idea how brightly you shine and how far your light reaches, but that's only because it is a light that comes from within. And even the sun doesn't know what it is to feel sunlight on its face, but that doesn't stop it from shining on.

That light in you hasn't gone out. You only *think* it has.

And the truth is, the world needs more lights just like you. ▮

SLOW GROWTH PRAYER

GOD,

This journey has been both a moment and a lifetime in the making. We have fought our way here to stand in this spacious ground, these dirt paths and green pastures spreading out before us at the edge of our After.

There is nothing left for us in our Before—only striving and spinning and achieving. And we're NOT going back.

As we stand before you, at last exhausted from all this running from our own stories, we hand it all over to you, God. Every good gift turned around and given right back to you.

"The use of my gifts . . . in service to others . . . for the rest of my life . . . for your ultimate glory." That's it.

I have my mission, now. I know my assignment. There are no more tightropes for me to walk, no more masked performances, no more splitting the difference of being tethered to you and tethered to a life lived only for myself.

I'm ALL in, God. Finally I can see all the places where the light gets in. And in this moment I decide:

This is the story I'll tell.

AMEN.

WE ARE STANDING
ON THE PRECIPICE
OF OUR AFTER.

growth equals strong roots.

OW
W

the nature of our it before having

NO 1

WALK AMONG THE
FIREFLIES

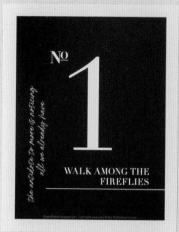

THE

PRELUDE

At a certain point, you stop running.

Breathless and at last exhausted, you double over at the pain of a lifetime spent proving. You've run so hard, for so long, you've gone so far out into the world. Only to keep finding yourself back at the beginning. You have spent a lifetime starting over, breaking loose to run free only to be taken captive again and again. This one truth always dragging, always clawing at your heels like the heavy chains you never asked to bear: no matter how hard you run, you can't outrun you.

So you crawl there for a while, panting through the pain, and then you curl up in surrender and rest your face on the cool, hard ground. Death to this old life you once knew. A mourning of what was lost, before the thrill of hope takes flight. A dying of self to become a new thing. This time, one with both roots and wings.

"God set me free, of me."

THE BOOK DIRT

"WE'RE ALL
JUST TRYING
TO FIND
OUR WAY
BACK HOME."

IAN MORGAN CRON

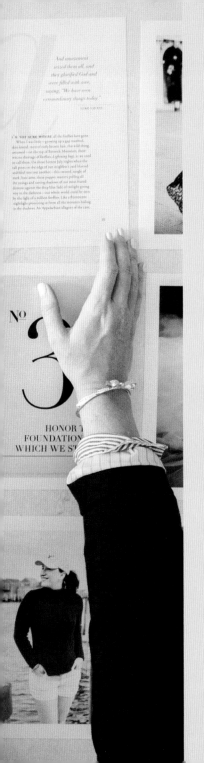

THE ACKNOWLEDGMENTS

PULLING OFF a book like this, where it is not just the words but every detail of every page that counts, takes nothing short of a dream team. And I just so happen to be someone who gets to wake up every day and work with the most wildly talented group of people, creating something that is not merely beautiful for the sake of being beautiful but that leaves others better for having found it. The kind of truth that points people back to Jesus, where true freedom is found.

Every day I get to wake up and walk amongst these giants. And I am forever better because of it.

Thank you to every single person at Baker Publishing Group and Revell for putting your entire heart and hard work into dreaming up this book alongside me and bringing it out into the world. To Kelsey Bowen for championing this book from start to finish, until every last detail was right. I am forever grateful to call you not only my editor but one of my very best friends. To William Overbeeke for taking my love of bold typography and editorial photography and turning it into one of the most beautiful interiors I have ever seen in a book. And to Laura Klynstra for designing the most beautiful cover to go with it! You both astound me! To Amy Nemecek for caring about these words as much as I do, calling me up to the highest standard, and making sure every last letter was right. I am a better writer because of how you use your gifts in the world. To Andrea Doering, Jennifer Leep, and Rachel McRae for your invaluable guidance in figuring out what this book was really about. And to Eileen Hanson, Wendy Wetzel, and Melissa Anschutz for shouting this book from the rooftops. Every single one of you puts the DREAM in our team, and I am the luckiest because of it.

To my own team, Elizabeth Evans, Dahlia Orth, and Allison Mari. You complete me. (And nothing would ever get done without you!) To my incredible agents, Jenni Burke and Marty Raz of Illuminate Literary Agency, thank you for the bright lights you both are in this world. To my coach-turned-friend Kim Butler, thank you for always cutting through the icing on top to get right to the crumbly center. The world is so much better because you stood firm in your place on the shore. And to our friends Erin and Peter, thank you for always reminding us to slow down and notice the fireflies.

To our styled shoot dream team for the many versions of "the woman who is always performing": Beth Chapman, DD Nickel, Erin Infantino, and our model-turned-muse herself, Kathryn Avery Myers, for being pure poetry in motion . . . thank you for everything! You all bring beauty and light to everything you do. And we are just lucky enough to be there to push the button. And to the one and only Abby Grace Springmann and Katherine Bignon, for working tirelessly to bring the styled shoot of me together so beautifully. You are both artists at what you do, and there is no one else I would have trusted!

To Justin, my partner in both photography and life, you are the most gifted artist I have ever known. You are a painter with light and you see the world unlike anyone else. The fact that you do it all with such humility just makes me love you all the more. Thank you for being the first one to ever tell me slow growth equals strong roots, and thank you for the past fifteen years of faithfully showing up to remind me whenever I am tempted to forget. Our roots now twist and turn into one another in such a way that I'm not sure where I end and you begin. And I wouldn't have it any other way.

Finally, thank you to every single reader who holds these pages. I pray that as you close this book, you would know just how deeply loved you are by God . . . without ever having to do a thing to earn it. I pray right now, as you are arriving at this place of at last exhausted, that you would realize your greatest contribution never came from showing up as The Most Put-Together Woman in the Room . . . it was always about you showing up in honesty and vulnerability, just as you are. This muddy story of yours has never once disqualified you—it is in fact your superpower. And the place where your gifts meet your story has the power to change lives.

As you move forward, be gentle with yourself. Overachieving is not something we give up once and then stop forever. Like anything we've become addicted to, it's a choice we have to make over and over. One day at a time.

I'm cheering for you. Always.

MARY MARANTZ grew up in a trailer in rural West Virginia. The first of her immediate family to go to college, she went on to earn a master's degree in moral philosophy and a law degree from Yale. After she turned down six-figure-salary law firm offers in London and New York, Mary and her husband, Justin, started a photography business, where they were named one of the prestigious Profoto Legends of Light. Together they have gone on to build a successful online education platform for thousands of creative entrepreneurs worldwide.

The bestselling author of *Dirt*, which was a 2021 Christian Book Award finalist, Mary is also the host of the highly ranked podcast *The Mary Marantz Show*, which debuted in the iTunes Top 200. Her work has been featured in *Business Insider*, *Bustle*, *Thrive Global*, *Southern Living*, *Hallmark Home & Family*, and more. She and Justin live in an 1880s fixer-upper by the sea in New Haven, Connecticut, with their two very fluffy golden retrievers, Goodspeed and Atticus. Learn more at MaryMarantz.com.

CONNECT WITH
MARY!

Helping world shakers own the
muddy parts of their stories

For speaking inquiries and to join the community, head to

MaryMarantz.com

  @marymarantz
#SlowGrowthEqualsStrongRoots

If you enjoyed reading *Slow Growth Equals Strong
Roots*, please help others discover it by leaving a
review online wherever books are sold! And share
your favorite quote or image from the book on your
social media account, tagging @MaryMarantz and
using hashtag #SlowGrowthEqualsStrongRoots.

The

MARY

MARANTZ SHOW

SLOW GROWTH *equals* STRONG ROOTS

Listen each week as host Mary Marantz brings
you honest conversations and offers her best tips
for business, relationships, faith, goals, and more.
Enter a space where you own the muddy parts of
your story and build things that matter. A space
where slow growth always equals strong roots.

TUNE IN AT
TheMaryMarantzShow.com

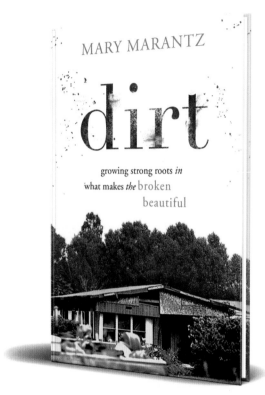